NEIL PEART: CULTURAL REPERCUSSIONS

NEIL PEART: CULTURAL REPERCUSSIONS

REVISED AND EXPANDED EDITION A FULL EXAMINATION OF THE WORDS AND IDEAS OF NEIL PEART, MAN OF LETTERS AND DRUMMER EXTRAORDINAIRE OF THE ROCK BAND RUSH.

BRADLEY J. BIRZER

Neil Peart: Cultural Repercussions
Revised and Expanded Edition
Copyright © 2022 Bradley J. Birzer
Previous edition published 2015

All rights reserved. No part of this book may be reproduced or transmitted in any form or by any electronic or mechanical means, including photocopying, recording or by any information storage and retrieval system, without the express written permission of the copyright holder, except where permitted by law.

The sole purpose of these materials is to educate and entertain. Although every precaution was taken to verify the accuracy of the information contained in this book, the author and publisher assume no responsibility for any errors or omissions. Any perceived slights to specific organizations or individuals are unintentional. No liability is assumed for damages that may result from the use of information contained in this book.

EBook ISBN: 978-1-68057-300-8
Trade Paperback ISBN: 978-1-68057-299-5

Cover design by Janet McDonald
Cover photo by Kelly Drew
Kevin J. Anderson, Art Director
Published by
WordFire Press, LLC
PO Box 1840
Monument CO 80132

Kevin J. Anderson & Rebecca Moesta, Publishers
WordFire Press eBook Edition 2022
WordFire Press Trade Paperback Edition 2022
WordFire Press Hardcover Edition 2022
Printed in the USA

Join our WordFire Press Readers Group for
sneak previews, updates, new projects, and giveaways.
Sign up at wordfirepress.com

DEDICATION

*Dedicated to Kevin McCormick,
"the most endangered species, the honest man."*

Some lives can be summed up in a sentence or two.
Other lives are epics.

—*Clockwork Lives* by Kevin J. Anderson and Neil Peart

INTRODUCTION

A Voice for an Entire Generation

Fittingly, and with no small sense of justice, the novel *Clockwork Angels*—based on the Rush album of the same name—became a *New York Times* bestseller on September 12, 2012, Neil Ellwood Peart's sixtieth birthday. His close friend and coauthor, science fiction writer Kevin J. Anderson, had the pleasure of informing the Canadian drummer and man of letters of their achievement in his annual birthday greetings.

The success of *Clockwork Angels* is not limited merely to the sales of the novel. The story originated in Peart's mind over a considerable period of time, with parts of it appearing in song form in 2010 as two singles, each performed on the 2011 Time Machine Tour. The full-length Rush album *Clockwork Angels* was released in the first half of June 2012. It was the nineteenth studio album of original material made by the progressive rock trio. The band toured extensively throughout North America and Europe to support the album, and a live version of the tour, simply entitled *Clockwork Angels: Tour*, came out on November 19, 2013. On that tour, the band played most of the album, complete with an elaborate stage, lighting, and set pieces, all serving to tell a better story. Rush had even hired a string ensemble to play with them. On Rush's last tour, R40 (summer 2015), the band continued to support the album, beginning the first set with three songs from *Clockwork Angels*.

That a novel appeared in the wake of a rock album is relatively exceptional. Most albums remain albums, though a few, such as Pink Floyd's *The Wall* and The Who's *Tommy* have become movies. Coheed and Cambria have released novels as well as comics to accompany their immense multi-album space opera, but they remain a cult band, at best. Through Peart's coauthor and close friend Anderson, the progressive metal band Roswell Six has released albums based on two of Anderson's novels in his Terra Incognita series.[1]

Clockwork Angels, though, has now appeared in the public eye as an album, a novel, an audiobook (with Peart himself, narrating it), a series of comic books, and a graphic novel. Even more impressively, one can purchase the audiobook in a variety of formats, including one that comes in a box designed to look like a clock tower (in which the clock actually functions).

Peart and Anderson penned a sequel, *Clockwork Lives*.[2] It, too, appeared in book format, as an audiobook (with an ensemble cast of readers), and as a graphic novel. If anything, the sequel is even better than the original. Filled with wisdom, pathos, and humor, *Clockwork Lives* grips the reader from the opening to the last page. A set of sturdy and attractive tarot-like cards were even produced to accompany the novel. And, the very book of *Clockwork Lives* is a thing of beauty, bound in red faux leather and adorned with alchemical symbols.

As of this writing, the third book of the Clockwork trilogy, *Clockwork Destiny*—plotted together before Peart's death in 2020—is moving into the production stage.

While no plans for a movie version yet exist, the story would certainly make an epic theater release or a long and involved series for television. The Clockwork universe is rich and diverse, full of possibilities, full of creativity, and full of potential.

Just like Peart himself was.

Indeed, the Clockwork universe might very well be the best allegory possible for the life, intellect, and soul of Neil Ellwood Peart, 1952–2020. He possessed immense talent. He was always a moving target, never satisfied with second best. His art—whether in lyrics, drumming, or prose—consistently built upon the past, always improving. He was in the fullest sense an individual, but he also almost always worked in small communities —whether with Geddy Lee and Alex Lifeson, or with Anderson, or with his motorcycling companions.

And, while Peart had no problem acknowledging his successes of the past, he was never content living there.

The past definitely has its place: behind me! But seriously, the only "stance" I have ever taken against the past is to say that now is better than then, and just as I dislike all delusions, I dislike nostalgia, which is just dressing up the past in sentimentality. (A quality, as Paul Theroux pointed out in The Happy Isles of Oceania, *which is too often displayed by bullies and boors.) Anybody whose life actually used to be good and now is bad, and they only expect it to get worse, well, they have my sympathy, for there's obviously something seriously wrong.*[3]

When asked what tunes Rush might play on their 1996–1997 *Test for Echo* tour, he admitted that many of the band's older songs made him squirm. "Do you want to see your kindergarten paintings hanging on the refrigerator?" he asked, only slightly in jest. "That's tough, to know that things you did 23, 24 years ago are still out there in front of people. Of course, it's embarrassing."[4]

Conversely, he felt great about *Clockwork Angels*. "It also seems natural that we always feel strongest about our newest music—like the soon-to-be released *Clockwork Angels* album. Yet people will keep asking me, 'What is your favorite Rush album?' How terrible it would be if you had to answer with anything *but* your most recent work."[5] And, perhaps to confirm just how highly Peart thought of Rush's nineteenth studio album, he announced he would soon retire from being a full-time member of the band, hoping to spend more time with wife and daughter. He also suffered from chronic tendonitis, which only worsened as Peart continued into his 60s.[6]

As with anyone, one hopes, Peart continued to progress in terms of interests, knowledge, wisdom, and skill throughout his life. He told the *Huffington Post* in late 2014:

I'm learning all the time. I'm evolving all the time as a human being. I'm getting better, I hope, in all of the important ways. So if I were less in the past it would be sad. It's like when people ask me my favorite record, my favorite Rush album. How horrible it would be if I had to say something from thirty years ago. How embarrassing, right? Well I did something good thirty years ago but it's been pretty much downhill since. No, no! I couldn't live with that![7]

This was not a new attitude for Peart. In a 1992 conversation hosted by the online site *The National Midnight Star*, he responded to a question about the source of inspiration for the "Fountain of Lamneth" on *Caress of Steel*: "Oh get off here. It's 1975, it's meaningless."[8] While Peart probably responded somewhat tongue-in-cheek, there's certainly a powerful element of truth in what he said.

Most men in the United States and Canada—especially those between the ages of forty and seventy-five (as of 2022)—know something about Peart. This is not to suggest that women do not like Rush, but it has been a running joke since the first concerts in the 1970s, that Rush primarily attracts men, though this has changed considerably over the past decade or so. In his book, *Far and Away*, Peart commented:

In a somewhat lighter vein, here's a bit of advice that Alex, Geddy, and I were joking about during an intermission one night, and agreed ought to be passed along: Guys, if your girlfriend hates Rush, don't bring her to the show. And if you absolutely have to bring her, buy her earplugs. At two of those British venues we looked out all night at a scowling female, front-row center, each with her fingers in her ears for the whole show. Hardly inspiring, for them or us![9]

Regardless, Peart is known first and foremost as the drummer and lyricist for Rush, having been a part of the band continuously since the second half of 1974. Depending on his age and from what part of the US or Canada he hails, a man will remember and feel nostalgia for "Fly by Night," "Closer to the Heart," "The Spirit of Radio," "Tom Sawyer," and "Subdivisions." These songs played in constant rotation throughout the late 1970s and 1980s on rock and AOR (Album Oriented Rock) stations across North America, especially in the area defined as the "Midwest." From Cleveland to Detroit, to Chicago, to Minneapolis/St. Paul, to Omaha and Lincoln, to Kansas City and Wichita, to Tulsa and Oklahoma City, and to every major city in Texas, Rush provided the soundtrack for high schoolers from the mid-1970s to the mid-1990s. And perhaps even more importantly, as Rush grew, their fan base grew with them.

From this lowest common denominator of knowledge among American and Canadian middle-aged men, the understanding of Peart, his abilities, and his ideas only rises, often to exponential proportions. Those who love Peart do so with a fervor generally reserved only for professionals in major league sports.

Descriptive terms arise readily when one thinks of Peart: authentic, professional, determined, tenacious, talented, intelligent, ingenious, adventurous, precise, perfectionistic, athletic, mischievous. He was a father, husband, drummer, writer, motorcyclist, hiker, explorer, dreamer, misfit, bibliophile, philosopher, ethicist, wordsmith, bicyclist, sailor, traveler, teacher, friend, and cultural critic. Ultimately, he was both an individual and an individualist. He may well have been one of the most interesting and influential persons of the last half century.

That he cherished his privacy and disdained the spotlight only makes his admirers respect him more. He didn't do what he did for any of us, necessarily, and he would certainly never have wanted a single member of his fandom to believe he or she has a claim on any aspect of him. Truly, he was not for rent to any god, government, group, or individual. He did what he did because it was the right thing to do and because he wanted those who follow his work to see that "care has been taken."

I don't believe any figure of the last half century has understood my generation any better than did Peart (except, perhaps, for John Hughes). It is, of course, nearly impossible to measure or quantify the influence that Peart wielded over so many over the past four decades. As a member of Rush, Neil Peart had served as the drummer and lyricist since 1974. We could measure album sales, book sales, concert appearances, etc. But in the end, the influence of one person on another is nearly incalculable. Unless someone states rather directly that this or that person has shaped him or her, we can only guess, sometimes well and sometimes poorly. We also cannot determine to what extent a person's words have affected another. What a listener hears, absorbs, and makes his own might not—in any, way, shape, or form—be what the originator intended. It might also not be obvious at any level. This is not a problem unique to Peart. It's as true for Socrates, Cicero, J.R.R. Tolkien, and Willa Cather as it was for Peart. Since Peart's death in January 2020, myriad tributes have been forthcoming, a sort of avalanche of good will, fondness, and admiration. The town of St. Catharines in Canada is even rededicating Lakeside Park to Peart as a permanent memorial.[10] The praise, which would have embarrassed him to no end, has been genuine and extensive.

When I saw Rush in concert in Auburn Hills, Michigan, in the fall of 2012, the huge crowd did not surprise me. Probably 80–90 percent male in composition, most of the audience ranged from ages thirty-five to sixty-five. Many, however, had their sons and even grandsons with them as well. As is typical for a post-1980 Rush crowd, every concert goer was exceedingly polite, friendly, and intensely interested. Though for only four or so hours (arrival until departure), we formed a community of like-minded people, all there to celebrate what Rush had so graciously bequeathed to and upon us for decades. That Rush could still draw thousands upon thousands of fans to their individual concerts after four decades of playing is also astounding. Rush lasted far longer than most businesses, some corporations, several countries, and even some religions. They were not playing in some small club in Nevada to a few die-hard fans. They possess a fan base as large and as devotedly loyal as almost any in music history. Critics—especially from establishment magazines in the US and the UK, such as *Rolling Stone* and *New Music Express*—have jeered them for years, but Rush as a band outlasted almost all of the critics. Though *Rolling Stone* has trashed Rush time and again, the magazine finally seems to have relented in its abuse, making the band its cover story in June 2015, and following, in great detail, the outpouring of good will upon Peart, after his death. Indeed, as if to erase all the nastiness of the past, *Rolling Stone* ran a beautiful article, a digital exclusive, entitled "The Spirit of Neil Peart," on the one-year anniversary of his death. It detailed the last three and a half years of Peart's life, focusing on his brain tumor and his stoic response to yet another tragedy in his life.[11]

Over the last forty-plus years, at least as many reviewers, if not more, have praised the band as have condemned it. What makes the negative critics so powerful is how much hatred and bitterness they spewed at the band, and especially at Peart. First, critics disliked that Peart was his own man and did not pander to them. He never did, nor can one imagine him ever having done so. Second, they hated that Peart comes out of the European tradition of music and writing, thus seemingly antagonistic to the Blues and the Blues basis of American rock. And third, they believed Peart's view of the world to have been destructive, as it was individualist and libertarian, thus associated with selfishness and social isolation.

Peart did not speak to the critics, at least not normally. He spoke to his own integrity, to those he respected, and to his fans. Peart never sought conformity but rather hoped to leaven the best in his listeners and readers. That is, Peart's excellence spoke to our excellences. He spoke to us.

I first encountered Rush in the detention section of the Liberty Junior High library in Hutchinson, Kansas, on the edge of spring, 1981. John Hinckley was days from shooting the fortieth president of the United States, the North American economy reeked, and my oldest brother was two months from earning his undergraduate degree from the University of Notre Dame. I was thirteen, and I'd done something (I don't remember what) to earn seventh-grade detention. While there, two fellow detainees—Brad and Troy—introduced me to *Moving Pictures*. Neil Peart and Rush have been a constant in my life ever since. When I first wrote these words, I had just returned from the second show of the R40 tour. My two oldest children and I made the pilgrimage to Lincoln, Nebraska, to see the three play their hearts out. And they did.

In this book, I examine the words and mind of Neil Peart. While Peart's words have affected me uniquely, I am certainly not unique in being affected. Indeed, by writing this book, I believe I speak for at least one generation of North American males and, more likely, for several.

—Brad Birzer, Hillsdale, Michigan
January 22, 2022

In this book, three things should be noted. First, although I am trained as a professional historian and academic scholar, I never really even attempt objectivity in this book. I'm a huge Rush fan, and I'm more concerned with sharing this enthusiasm than I am in feigning a detached disinterest. I've done my best, of course, to be honest, but I'm not without my own passions, proudly expressed. As such, I can be intensely personal—such as with the loss of my daughter, Cecilia Rose—in this book.

Second, now that Neil Peart has passed away, I refer to him in the past tense, but I refer to his work (and the work of Rush) in the present tense, considering each album (and book) a living and dynamic work of art.

Third, I reference Rush albums according to genre and intent, but always chronologically. I believe that one can trace a continuity and a true progression from 1974 to 2015. In particular, I consider the Rush that emerged after Peart's twin tragedies of 1997 and 1998 to be a fulfillment of the band's potential, not a break from it.

I explain the following groupings throughout the course of the book.

Rush 1.0
Rush (Moon 1974)

Rush 2.0
Fly by Night (Mercury 1975)
Caress of Steel (Mercury 1975)
2112 (Mercury 1976)
A Farewell to Kings (Mercury 1977)
Hemispheres (Mercury 1978)

Rush 2.1
Permanent Waves (Mercury 1980)
Moving Pictures (Mercury 1981)
Signals (Mercury 1982)
Grace Under Pressure (Mercury 1983)
Power Windows (Mercury 1985)
Hold Your Fire (Mercury 1987)

Rush 2.2
Presto (Atlantic 1989)
Roll the Bones (Atlantic 1991)
Counterparts (Atlantic 1993)

Rush 2.3
Test for Echo (Atlantic 1996)

Rush 3.0
Vapor Trails (Atlantic 2002); *Vapor Trails Remixed* (Atlantic 2013)
Feedback (Atlantic 2004)
Snakes and Arrows (Atlantic 2007)
Clockwork Angels (Roadrunner 2012)

No one stage is a break from the past, but rather a betterment and fulfillment of the previous stage, whether represented by a full number or a mere decimal point.

---

1. Kevin J. Anderson, *The Edge of the World* (New York: Orbit, 2010); and Kevin J. Anderson, *The Map of All Things* (New York: Orbit, 2010). The corresponding Roswell Six albums are *Beyond the Horizon* and *A Line in the Sand*. Each also featured Anderson and his wife, Rebecca Moesta, as co-lyricists. Anderson dedicated *The Edge of the World* to Peart: "A friend for nearly twenty years, and his music has given me tremendous inspiration for much longer than that. Without those lyrics triggering a cascade of ideas, many of my stories would never have been conceived."
2. Kevin J. Anderson and Neil Peart, *Clockwork Lives* (ECW, 2015).
3. Steve Streeter, "Life on Paper!" *A Show of Fans* 17 (Summer 1997).

4. Brian McCollum, "Look Back?" *Philadelphia Inquirer* (November 6, 1996), pg. E4.
5. Peart, *Far and Near*, 92.
6. Martin Kielty, "Peart Pain is Part of Rush Road Retirement," *Classic Rock* (April 29, 2015), http://classicrock.teamrock.com/news/2015-04-29/rush-neil-peart-tendonitis-tour-retirement.
7. "Far and Near: An Interview with Neil Peart," *Huffington Post* (huffingtonpost.com), October 9, 2014.
8. Frank Lancaster, "An Interview with Neil Peart," *National Midnight Star* (April 23, 1992).
9. Peart, *Far and Away*, 32.
10. https://www.loudersound.com/news/lakeside-park-tribute-to-rushs-neil-peart-gets-green-light
11. Brian Hiatt, "The Spirit of Neil Peart," (Digital exclusive), *Rolling Stone* (January 7, 2021).

1 A MAN OF HIS WORDS
1974–1979

Born into a middle-class family in Ontario, Canada, Neil Peart found his love of the drums at age thirteen. At that point, "Everything disappeared," he remembered. "I'd done well in school up until that time. I was fairly adjusted socially up until that time." Once he started drum lessons, however, "I became completely monomania-obsessed all through my teens. Nothing else existed anymore."[1]

When Neil Peart joined Rush in 1974, the band had already released one album, the successful self-titled album with its best and most recognizable debut single, "Working Man." Not wanting to imitate Led Zeppelin too much, Geddy Lee and Alex Lifeson had already begun moving toward a much more progressive position musically while touring to support the first album. They still loved Zeppelin, The Who, Cream, Buffalo Springfield, and the Yardbirds, but they were also quite taken with what Yes, Genesis, and King Crimson were accomplishing, especially in the United Kingdom.

It's worth remembering that though the first two Rush albums appeared only eleven months apart, the first album had been in the works for almost five years by the time it came on the market. In those five years, Lee and Lifeson reached the age of 21

—no longer teenagers, but men. It stands to reason that those five years not only shaped them on a day-to-day level as they matured, but also exposed them to a radically different sound in rock as the music scene rapidly changed during the late 1960s and the first half of the 1970s.

The band's second album, *Fly by Night*—the first written with Peart—reveals a serious maturation of sound and confidence over the first album. While the debut album, *Rush*, had decent production and good hard, acid-rock-like riffs, it was, lyrically speaking, rather pedestrian. That is, it provided a great sound to accompany drinking beer with friends, driving around the countryside without too many worries, and pumping fists in the air.

The words, though, were far from heady and certainly less than extraordinary. *Rush* was little more than blues-acid-party-rock music for Midwestern teenagers to enjoy while drinking, smoking, and making out. This represents, as I have decided to label the pre-Peart Rush era, Rush 1.0. The contrast between this album and what Peart would contribute over the next forty years is startling.

Hey, baby, it's a quarter to eight
I feel I'm in the mood
Hey baby, the hour is late
I feel I've got to move

—"In the Mood" 1974

The lyrics of the first album prove as ephemeral as almost anything Foghat or Headeast wrote in that decade. They mean next to nothing, but they can call up wells of nostalgia for those who might have danced, drunk, smoked, or made out to such music as it first appeared on the pop scene. When Rush finished their R40 concert in Lincoln on May 10, 2015, with "Working Man," the crowd—a mostly middle-aged white male audience—went absolutely wild. While it's a great song, it simply cannot compare to the complexity of a "Tom Sawyer" or a "Headlong Flight." Still, "Working Man" captures the imaginations of its listeners, even after nearly five decades.

When Peart joined the band in the summer of 1974, Rush 2.0 began and would last until 1997. When Rush re-emerged after the horrific tragedies in Peart's life with *Vapor Trails* in 2002, they became the ultimate Rush, Rush 3.0.

While many would agree that Peart is one of the greatest drummers of all time, he might also justly be considered one of the best living essayists in the English language. Peart cherished the word, in whatever form. This proves equally true in his book and essay writing, his lyrics, and even in his interviews. A writer for the *Toronto Star* enthused: "Peart's verbal skills would be the envy of any politician. Grammatically structured sentences tumble from his mouth at a breathless rate without pauses, ums, or hesitations, as if his mouth is in perfect synch with a brain firing on all cylinders."[2] It's not, however, only his skills at communication. He cherished the opportunity to make those words incarnate, to give them tangible and physical form.

It occurred to me that there are few activities more enjoyable than making things. When I was young, it was car models, go-karts, then later pop-art mobiles and laughably inept carpentry. A couple of years ago, I ran across a wall-mount "drumstick holder" I had dreamed up in my teens. It had been inspired by my dad's cue rack by his pool table, but it was a crudely shaped assemblage of gray-painted plywood, with holes drilled by an old brace-and-bit — it looked like it had been crafted by a troglodyte. But still — I had made something. It is stimulating and satisfying to write stories, or play the drums, but most gratifying of all to me is creating a physical object: a book, a CD, a DVD. Of course it remains the content that gives the mere object its value, but many would agree, I hope, that owning such a carefully crafted object is more pleasing than just acquiring the content by whatever means. That urge may sustain the existence of things apart from their content, and that would be good, methinks.[3]

Peart, however, also longed to communicate with his audience, even if he usually preferred to maintain some distance from its individual members.

Communication is what music is, certainly. And the lyrics, and writing the bio, and basically every aspect of what we do, is essential communication. That it can't really be two-way, in the sense of communication, but it can be successful. It takes certainly two people to make it successful. If you're transmitting an idea, you need a receiver, and for that receiver, you need good media in between. So that's where the craft comes into it too, of carefully refining that idea, or that thought, or that feeling, so that it communicates to a listener.[4]

Certainly, Peart and his two bandmates hoped to connect with the best and the most intelligent of their audience.

Words can carry different freight for different people, of course, but for those who do have the sensitivity to pay the kind of attention to lyrics I put into them, it's wonderful to connect that way. To feel that you're not playing down to anyone. We've always had the impression that people are just as smart as we are. If we can figure this stuff out, they can too ... This is really what turned us on this year. Lyrically, it's always been a reflection of my times and the times I observe.[5]

He also had no problem directly talking to those he considered equals or betters, whatever their own fields of expertise. That is, Peart maintained a number of sustained, deep friendships. He was not, as some have claimed, anti-social. He distrusted those who admired him because of their own illusions and delusions, those who would project their own hopes and desires upon him. For those who listen to his music, however, Peart presented his case(s) in Socratic fashion.

But it's certainly true that we think about what we do. Our music is a reflection of our interest. It is made by thinking people for thinking people. We never talk down to our audiences. I presume they are as smart as we are. Anyone who knows us should have the perception that we work hard and enjoy it. We pay attention to the real details. We take care to imprint our set of values on it. The same values that apply to our music extend through our organization.[6]

Peart adamantly denied the label of preacher, however. Rather, he claimed that every thought he presented, he did so as a question, an invitation to enter a long-term conversation.[7] It was, he continued, nothing but a love and honesty of spirit. His own music heroes—such as Roger Waters, Joni Mitchell, Paul Simon, Ian Anderson, and Pete Townshend—always "cared about what they do." At some level, Peart continued, "I sensed what was honest, and I sensed when care had been taken, when someone really meant what they sang."[8]

Peart's lyrics on *Fly by Night*, though, took Rush to a whole new level of exploration and intellectual respectability. The opening moments of the album reveal a new Rush. In full defiance of the Aquarian norms of '60s rock, Peart offers an "Anthem," a statement of individualistic pride in one's creation and integrity, accompanied by pounding acidic bass and drums, driving the rhythm to levels and depths well beyond the pop norm of 4/4 time signatures.

Anthem of the heart and anthem of the mind
A funeral dirge for eyes gone blind
We marvel after those who sought
The wonders of the world, wonders of the world
Wonders of the world they wrought
Live for yourself ... there's no one else
More worth living for
Begging hands and bleeding hearts will only cry out for more.

While one might understandably define these lyrics as Social Darwinist, they are an attempt to define the individual—often lost as a part of a community in the Aquarian themes of '60s lyrics—in a positive, proactive manner. And, while not at the level of a Henry David Thoreau, they show significant depth relative to other lyrics of the day and especially considering this was reportedly twenty-two-year-old Peart's first attempt at writing. He would continue the same theme of perseverance in "Something for Nothing" and "Marathon."

Most of the songs on *Fly by Night* follow the traditional rock format in terms of length, ranging from just under 3 minutes to just under 7 minutes. One track, though, stands out in terms of structure, lyrics, and length, revealing the future direction of Rush, the bizarrely named "By-Tor and the Snow Dog." If the opening song revealed Peart's love of the individualism of nineteenth-century America, this song equally demonstrated his appreciation for the fantastical world of J.R.R. Tolkien. At 8½ minutes and broken into four parts, "By-Tor" tells the story of a demon from hell who attempts to open a portal to the Overworld. The champion of the latter, Snow Dog, defeats By-Tor in open combat, thus saving the world of the living from the twilight realm of the dead.

Fly by Night reveals Peart's uncanny ability to combine eighteenth-century Enlightenment philosophy—admittedly, a century or two after its time and glory—with the fantastic and mythic as understood in the twentieth century. While the opening track expresses a rugged individualism, By-Tor demonstrates that individual bravery can save an entire world as well as bring glory and honor upon the rescuer. These seemingly incompatible themes predominate in many of Peart's early lyrics.

Fly by Night, of course, began the career of a band that would continue with the same lineup for over four decades, an incredible achievement by any measure. In 2016, Lee reflected on exactly what it was that allowed the band to continue over so many years and through so many challenges.

That's the hardest question to answer. I'd like to say it has something to do with our extreme Canadian-ness. We're just too polite to be nasty to each other. Or maybe we're just too lacking in imagination to want a new set of girlfriends. There's a common sense of fairness that we share. And when you couple that with our sense of humour ... that's profound and overrides all practical considerations. I don't think you can get us in a room to discuss anything where we're serious for more than five minutes. I think that has a lot to do with it. And there's a musical respect for each other that's a huge part of the occasion. We all truly believe that we're better musicians together than we are separately.[9]

CARESS OF STEEL

A mere six months after releasing *Fly by Night*, Rush released their third LP—the second with Peart—*Caress of Steel*. In almost every way, *Caress* serves as a sequel to *Fly by Night*. But, if *Fly by Night* was the black sheep of the rock world, *Caress* was its estranged stoner cousin who only attended family events when someone had unexpectedly passed away. "I think we were pretty high when we made that record," Lee laments with a snicker, "and it sounds like it to me."[10] Looking back on the time, Lee admits that they had smoked too much hash oil, something the band would soon regret.[11] Just as "Anthem" begins with bass and drums in a blistering assault on the ears and an appeal to the ego, "Bastille Day" begins with guitar and bass, drums coming in only seconds behind, the guitar and bass playing an almost acid version of Wagnerian strings. If "Anthem" celebrated the dignity and integrity of the creative person, "Bastille Day" warned that those who assault the integrity of the individual would find themselves in a violent, untenable situation.

For the young Peart, the individual is natural and innovative, while the collective and its leaders corrupt and perverse. With the exception of the novelty rock song, "I Think I'm Going Bald," *Caress* is musically far superior to *Fly by Night*, despite the close ties between the two albums. For better or worse, Rush seems to have progressed so much with this third album that even the progressive rock world was unsure what do with it. Filled with a million ideas, each idea is pregnant, awaiting birth, light, and formation. "Lakeside Park" evokes nostalgia, and the final two tracks, each epic, return Rush firmly to the Tolkienian world of fantasy. Once again, *Caress* is an American Thoreau walking through Tolkien's Shire.

At 12½ minutes in length, the final track of side one, "The Necromancer," finishes the tale of By-Tor. In this incarnation of the story, Prince By-Tor serves the forces of good and light. As Lee recounts it, the band took the story with a grain of salt, believing it rather humorous.[12] Still, the band took the music very seriously. According to Lifeson:

We wanted to work in a longer format, with more dynamics, quiet parts, loud parts. We were feeling the progressive movement of the time with Yes, Genesis, King Crimson, bands like that. We were becoming more sophisticated and complex in our arrangements, or at least trying to. We were still really young.[13]

Narrated in spoken word by Neil Peart, the story sees By-Tor challenge the Necromancer and his wraiths. Interestingly enough, By-Tor emerges in Middle-earth, perhaps to aid in the attack on Sauron. Why By-Tor has embraced the good is unclear, but it probably matters little. Rush expertly tell the story through bass, drums, and guitars. And Peart dedicates the song to TV fabulist, Rod Serling, and it ends with the Latin inscription, *Terminat hora diem; terminat auctor opus. (As the day ends, so ends the work of the author.)* The line comes from the grand Elizabethan playwright Christopher Marlowe, in his play *Dr. Faustus*, itself most likely influencing Shakespeare's *Macbeth* and certainly influenced by Machiavelli's *The Prince*. For Peart, the Latin served as a fitting tribute to Serling and his works of imagination and dark drama.[14]

The final song, "The Fountain of Lamneth," another epic at

20 minutes and with six parts, was the most "progressive" song Rush had yet written. Lush, it builds slowly and gently, but always with a steady determination. Rush successfully mixes the staccato of their best rhythms—as in "Anthem" and "Bastille Day"—with their more gentle ballads such as "Rivendell" from *Fly by Night*. As a whole, "Fountain" swings from delicate to punctuated, and it is probably the best song Rush had recorded to that point. Three things made it excellent. First, and most importantly, Peart was at his best in terms of lyric writing. As noted several times in this book, Peart loved the story of journeys, whether of his physical being or of his imagination. In this, Peart followed the western tradition of Homer, Virgil, Dante, and Tolkien. Lamneth's journey is: awakening and imagination, realization that authority adulterates creativity, departure from parents and teachers, ecstasy of freedom, the routine of freedom without creativity, and finally, a reawakening of imagination and spirit as a new journey begins. The second thing that made this song strong was that the music fit the story at every level and helped to tell it, augmenting the words with time signature changes and chord progressions. Third—something even Rush fans often miss—was the ability of Lee to pitch his voice perfectly to the story that Peart wrote. His voice, while perhaps not beautiful, is uniquely full of purpose and truth, especially in "Lamneth."

In 1975, Lee, Lifeson, and Peart believed they had created a masterpiece with this album, and in fact, they truly had. But their fans, present and future, were not yet ready for such a thing. Rush had advanced and developed too quickly for the genre, and the album failed commercially. In his famous 1942 lectures in Scotland, T.S. Eliot, a man whom Peart admired greatly, explained that the poet always runs the risk of developing more quickly than his audience, something that proved good neither for poet nor listener.

But there is one law of nature more powerful than any of these varying currents, or influences from abroad or from the past: the law that poetry must not stray too far from the ordinary everyday language which we use and hear. Whether poetry is accentual or syllabic, rhymed or rhyme-less, formal or free, it cannot afford to lose its contact with the changing language of common intercourse.[15]

Without doing violence to Eliot's meaning, one might even substitute his "varying currents" with "permanent waves."

Actually, *Caress of Steel* sold well, but it did so at the same level that the previous album, *Fly by Night*, had. Their record company, Mercury, had expected much more from the band.

Most critics either ignored *Caress* or mocked it. Their most important British advocate, Geoff Barton, lamented:

I played the latest (and admittedly rather derivative) Rush album "Caress of Steel" in the office the other day, and unfortunately it received howls of derision. Young lead singer/bassist Geddy Lee sounds like Robert Plant and Burke Shelley combined and guitarist Alex Lifeson has his various rip-off offerings to a tee. But they make a pleasing sound and the band's Tolkien-oriented lyrics are well constructed.[16]

Unfortunately, Barton failed to elaborate. In what way was *Caress* derivative, one must ask? It does resemble some of Steve Hackett's work with Peter Gabriel–era Genesis, but it remains very Lifeson-esque.[17] The only part of the entire album that fit into the music scene of 1975 was part five, "Bacchus Plateau." Tellingly, it is the part of the story that mocks conformity to trends, intentionally sounding like every rock song of that year. Obviously, this not-so-subtle subtlety was lost on the reviewers. Interestingly, the protagonist wakes up from his conformity by drinking "another goblet from the cask of '43." While Peart did not specify, he likely was referring to Ayn Rand's best novel, *The Fountainhead*, published that year. Rand (1905–1982), a Russian-

American immigrant, novelist, and philosopher, plays an important role in the life of Peart and Rush, and she will be discussed in more detail momentarily in this book.

David Brown of *Record Mirror* understood the album best, but failed to review it until a year and a half after its initial release. In February 1977, he wrote:

While it is true they are not the only heavy rock storytellers, they manage to carry it off with a higher degree of conviction than most. In Alex Lifeson they have a guitarist capable of expressing every mood from calm to terror, and while there are, as with his companions, a few clichés (as in the song "I Think I'm Going Bald" with its "Now we're so involved, so involved with life"), the overall feel is what really counts.[18]

The band began to feel the weight of its critics on the tour supporting the album, and they began to refer to it as the "Down the Tubes" tour, traveling with Ted Nugent and performing for smaller and smaller audiences. Whatever their own personal feelings, they played their hearts out. As a Canadian program described them:

And yet the critics hate them. Too loud. Too noisy. Not settled. And Geddy Lee and Alex Lifeson and Neil Peart keep on moving, keep on turning audiences on, keep on laughing—at the critics, and at themselves. The trio takes music seriously, but they enjoy their life, and it shows on stage, when the music begins. Yes, it is loud, much of it— although, increasingly, Rush is finding that its audience can and does get into the quieter, serious stuff. Yes, Geddy Lee does have a voice like his throat is full of razor blades. Yes, Alex Lifeson's guitar playing is loud and could remind you of a jackhammer, but it's also fast and clean and smooth. And, yes, Neil Peart—towel draped around his neck—has to be one of the most powerful drummers rock has turned up yet.[19]

Granted, the above was a work of promotion and public relations, but it rings true to the history of the band and the integrity of its members.

Musician and artist Hugh Syme created the cover for *Caress of Steel*. While the production of this cover was his first introduction to Rush, Syme quickly became a vital part of the band, being, for all intents and purposes, the band's visual spokesman. His packaging, fonts, layouts, and sets were the means by which Rush presented themselves to the public in any medium beyond sound. Syme remains the main graphic artist and designer for the band to this day. He has designed every album, every DVD/Blu-Ray, every tour book, and every book the band has released since 1975. He has also played keyboards on three Rush songs. For forty years, he has been responsible for the Rush image as much as anyone outside of the three actual members of the band.

As noted in the appendix to this book, Roger Dean is probably a "prettier" artist than Syme. Syme is, however, far more interesting and diverse. If Dean offers sameness and similarity of theme throughout his many album covers, Syme satisfies curiosity and has taken innumerable chances in all of his endeavors. He's bold and audacious in every aspect of his art. He's quirky, as well. Whether it's a "natural" font on *Signals* or a precise graphic for *Clockwork Angels*, Syme delivers. In other words, he's perfect for Rush and for Peart. "From the first time Hugh and I met we shared a level of communication that would sustain us through all the years of discussing art by long distance," Peart recalled. "We had the same value and tastes in images and design, and simply *spoke the same language*."[20] Whatever went wrong with *Caress of Steel*, the alliance between Peart and Syme for the art and design of that album made up for all other ills.[21]

2112

Peart remembered what a difficult and yet critical time it was for the band after disappointing Mercury with *Caress of Steel*. The band immediately had to make a number of decisions, few of them pleasant.

The band's first, self-titled album had been recorded just before I joined, and when it sold 125,000 copies in the United States, the record company pronounced it "a promising debut." When the next one, Fly by Night, sold 125,000 copies, it was "a solid follow-up." But when the third album, Caress of Steel, sold 125,000 copies, they called it "a dog." We were urged to be "more commercial," write some "singles." So, in our contrarian fashion, we recorded an ambitious and impassioned sidelong piece about a futuristic dystopia, along with a few other weird songs, and released our fourth album, 2112, early in 1976. It was considered by the bean counters to be our last chance, and without any promotion from them, it was something of a snowball's chance.[22]

Caress ended on an organic, open and free-spirited note, but *2112* began with discordant and spacey computer noises and swatches of sound. The contrast in mood and sound could not have been greater. *2112* even inverted the structure of *Caress*, placing the epic sidelong track on side one of the album, with the shorter songs on side two.

Again, it's worth remembering that if they were going to end, they were going to do so on their own terms. If Rush was going "down the tubes," they were going to go down with a serious statement and a very, very loud thud. No whimper. Only a bang. "We talked about how we would rather go down fighting rather than try to make the kind of record they wanted us to make," Lee remembers. "We made *2112* figuring everyone would hate it, but we were going to go out in a blaze of glory."[23] Lifeson feels the same. "*2112* is all about fighting the man," he states. "Fortunately for us, that became a marker. That was also the first time that we really started to sound like ourselves."[24]

It is hard to judge whether or not this anti-authoritarian streak in Rush came from the group as a whole or from each of the three individuals who made up the band. Perhaps the distinction is irrelevant.

While one might readily and honestly label Lee, Lifeson, and Peart as individualists, it is because of Peart's words that he might also have been one of the greatest living exponents—in word and deed—of individualism itself. Yet, his individualism was far from selfish, as he desired every person in the world to be such. "I call myself an individualist because no-one knows what that means either—except me. So if anyone asks me to put an 'ism' after my name I'll say I'm an individualist because to me an individual life is the ultimate, supreme-value in the world."[25] Peart disliked "authority of all kinds," but especially the righteous authority wielded by governments, churches, and "moral majorities."[26] As a whole, Rush had remained "implicitly and explicitly rebellious," the drummer believed. "We demand to do it our way, even if we are wrong. We resist the machine and we refuse to be mercenary."[27] Sounding very much like fabulist J.R.R. Tolkien and a number of other humanists and artists of the twentieth century, Peart stated, with great enthusiasm and relish, that he loves the individual because "each person is a story."[28]

As the strange science fiction swirls fade, the opening to *2112*, an anthem begins. Not an anthem in the sense of *Fly by Night's* "Anthem," but an anthem of battle and victory, a struggle of the individual against the tyrant. The *2112* overture drives relentlessly toward victory. Harkening back to the *1812 Overture*, the *2112* overture captivated most listeners—especially considering that many Rush fans at the time were in their teens and twenties and almost always male—and they would've gleefully banged their heads and raised their fists. Rock music does not come more martial and victorious than this. The story of *2112*, based loosely on Ayn Rand's 1938 science fiction novella *Anthem* and Yevgeny Zamyatin's *We*, presents a dystopian short story. Through a series of catastrophes and apocalypses, Earth exists no more, and humans have migrated into the universe. The protagonist of *2112* lives more or less without the ability or will to question in a totalitarian-collectivist society ruled by Philosopher-priests who proclaim their own power and control in very loud dramatic fashion. In their powers, they resemble the most stringent rulers of Plato's *Republic* and, in their voices, they sound akin to the Pharisees of *Jesus Christ Superstar*. The protagonist discovers an "ancient miracle," a guitar. Gifted musically, he learns to play it, discovering a way to bring real beauty into a closed society. Naively, the protagonist assumes the Philosopher-priests simply did not know about the instrument. Otherwise, in their supposed wisdom, he presumes, still naive, they would have already adopted it and promoted it within the larger society. Seeing no utility in the guitar, the Philosopher-priests forbid its usage, presuming it a toy. Additionally, they claim that it helped destroy the pre-interstellar-migration elder race of man. Distraught, the protagonist takes the Stoic route, killing himself rather than accepting continued life in a world devoid of such glories as music. "I don't think I can carry on, carry on this cold and empty life." *2112* ends with the suicide, a return to the overture theme, and, in an ending sometimes contested by the fans, representatives of the glorious elder race return in great numbers and announce—with loudness and confidence—that they have "assumed control." At the time Peart, who developed the entire concept and story, viewed the ending as "a real Hitchcock killer."[29]

To this day, more than four decades after the release of *2112*, Neil Peart has never fully shaken the "Ayn Rand" label. For those who love Rand, Peart stands as a hero for upholding her ideals, in spirit and in word. For those who despise Rand, Peart's reference to her remains a black mark on the history of the Canadian power trio, forever condemning Rush to the status of "right-wing rock" at best and "fascist" at worst. When the accusations flew, the members of Rush were stunned. Lifeson remembered:

I think that it was misconstrued by the right to mean that we were more in that mind-set. The tougher press was the English press, the left-wing press, like New Musical Express *at the time in the '70s. They thought we were fascists. Ha ha. But there's barely a political bone in our bodies. We were just telling a story about a guy who finds a guitar and he's standing up to The Man.*[30]

The British press, especially "were calling us 'junior fascists' and 'Hitler lovers,'" Peart remembered. "It was a total shock to me."[31] At best, Peart considered himself "an apolitical person really."[32]

Economist and man of letters Steven Horwitz had done the best job of analyzing the influence of Rand on Peart, while Rob Freedman showed how this led to horrendous accusations being thrown at the drummer, such as a supposed proclivity toward fascism (an idea so ridiculous as to be completely offensive).

Whatever Rand was, she was quite the opposite of a fascist in her ideas and ideals, though she did possess a rather strong Nietzschean streak in her writings, as did Peart. Famous mostly for her perennially bestselling novels *Atlas Shrugged* and *The Fountainhead*, Rand also authored numerous nonfiction essays and books, including a number that upheld the idea of selfishness as a virtue. She took the right to self-ownership and personal property to the *n*th degree, believing that selflessness denied nature as well as the dignity of the creative and free individual. Charity, she feared, if forced, diminished the very being of the individual. Rand even took this to the level of love and sexual relationships, seeing the two lovers as writing (for lack of a better term) a type of mutually self-interested contract with one another. Her sex scenes, which many critics have described as barely concealed rape, embrace a sort of domination of the superior partner over the less superior partner. Though few critics have offered even a semblance of balance when discussing Rand—either loving or hating her—her students and followers, such as Doug Den Uyl, Aeon Skoble, Yaron Brook, Bradley Thompson, and David Mayer offer some of the most interesting scholarship available. They are honest, interesting, and logical to a rigorous degree.

Peart's sin, if it can be considered as such, was that he openly thanked Rand, dedicating *2112* to her "genius."[33] Though Peart offered the dedication through his direct writing, he spoke for the band as a whole, as each of the three members had read and enjoyed Rand's science fiction novella *Anthem*.[34] A year later, he admitted that his two great literary heroes were Rand's two major protagonists: Howard Roark of *The Fountainhead* and John Galt of *Atlas Shrugged*.[35] What is unfortunate, at least in terms of Peart's long-term reputation, is that for roughly four decades now, allies and enemies of Rush have latched onto this obvious and blatant dedication and his brief support of Rand. Not atypically, *Rolling Stone* seized on Peart's Randianism with a vengeance, using it as yet one more thing to hate about the band. In a review of *Exit ... Stage Left*, Jon Pareles screeched:

Just about everything Rush do can be found, more compactly, in Yes' "Roundabout," with the remainder in Genesis' "Watcher of the Skies." Everything except the philosophy—and stage left is, of course, to the audience's far right.[36]

Why an audience far to the *left* of Rush remained so loyal to the band, made absolutely no sense, but few read the mainstream music magazine for logic. Certainly, Rand shaped the young Peart dramatically, as she has shaped so many others of the same age for well over half a century now. In 1971, while living in London, Peart found a discarded copy of Rand's *The Fountainhead* in the tube station.[37]

To a 20-year-old struggling musician, The Fountainhead was a revelation, an affirmation, an inspiration. Although I would eventually grow into and, largely, out of Ayn Rand's orbit, her writing was still a significant stepping-stone, or way-station, for me, a black-and-white starting point along the journey to a more nuanced philosophy and politics. Most of all, it was the notion of individualism that I needed—the idea that what I felt, believed, liked, and wanted was important and valid.[38]

Peart had said something similar to *MacLeans* (the Canadian equivalent of *Time* or *Newsweek*):

For me it was a confirmation of all the things I'd felt as a teenager. I had thought I was a socialist like everyone else seemed to—you know, why should anyone have more than anyone else?—but now I think socialism is entirely wrong by virtue of man himself. It cannot work. It is simply impossible to say all men are brothers or that all men are created equal—they are not. Your basic responsibility is to yourself.[39]

Again, in 1997, Peart reaffirmed this. "Howard Roark stood as a role model for me—as exactly the way I already was living," he stated in an interview with the libertarian magazine, *Liberty*. "And it was intuitive or instinctive or inbred stubbornness or whatever; but I had already made those choices and suffered for them."[40]

Of course, Peart was not the first or last North American twenty-something to find the ideas of Ayn Rand a justification for creativity, rebellion, and individualism. That Rand's novels have sold millions and millions of copies over the course of more than eight decades, demonstrates the lasting and singular appeal of her works.

Yet by 1977, Lee's "Cinderella Man" negated much of the most extreme aspects of Rand's philosophy of selfishness. When asked about the author's influence on the band in 1997, Lee responded: "only as [her views] pertained to the idea of artistic freedom. I'd have to say we were never very interested in the more extreme libertarianism of her politics."[41]

In the 1988 "Backstage Newsletter," Peart answered a fan question about the continuing influence of Rand on his own writing and understanding of the world. Peart answered:

Well, lately I'm never inspired by any one thing, and usually try to pour a bucketful of ideas and images into every song, so the actual inspirations can be pretty oblique and hard to track down. They come from conversations sometimes, or something in the newspaper or on TV, or more often just from watching the way people behave, and thinking about why![42]

In a 1992 interview, Lee again reflected on Rand's influence on the band, noting that while they had had an obsession with her, that obsession was long gone. "I think she had a great influence, her writing had a great influence on our work and it had a great influence on our lives, but more in a sense of her artistic manifesto and her belief in the ability of the individual to succeed. Art is a personal expression," Lee said. "Art is something done to satisfy oneself as opposed to art for the people, which is kind of an unexplainable phrase in itself. Art—you set the terms for your life. You set the terms for your art. I think those kind of things in her work have affected us and probably the residue of that has lingered through the years."[43]

When the question came up again from a fan in 1994, Peart offered a fairly detailed response.

For a start—the extent of my influence by the writings of Ayn Rand should not be overestimated—I am no one's disciple. Yes, I believe the individual is paramount in matters of justice and liberty, but in philosophy, as Aristotle said long ago, the paramount good is happiness. My self-determination as an individual is part of the pursuit of happiness, of course, but there's more to it than that.[44]

Peart was especially disgusted by those followers of Rand who had seemingly become obsequious automatons, losing their individuality in their desire to ape their master. "That was when I started to not become a Randroid, and started to part from being a true believer," Peart argued, noting that he disagreed with Rand over her treatment of Woodstock and over her legion of followers. By the early 1980s, he had cancelled his subscription to the Rand newsletter, *The Objectivist Forum*. "It's in the nature of the individualist ethos that you don't want to be co-opted."[45]

In a *National Midnight Star* interview in the first half of the 1990s, Peart labeled himself a "left-wing libertarian," thus negating any possibility of being a straightforward Rand-Objectivist. By 2007, Peart openly rejected Rand as a continuing influence in the Rush song, "Good News First," which blatantly mocked one of that Russian-American authoress's most important concepts, the notion of a "benevolent universe" as explored toward the end of this book. Most recently, Peart described himself as a "Bleeding-Heart Libertarian."

For me, it was an affirmation that it's all right to totally believe in something and live for it and not compromise. It was a simple as that. On that 2112 album, again, I was in my early twenties. I was a kid. Now I call myself a bleeding-heart Libertarian. Because I do believe in the principles of Libertarianism as an ideal—because I'm an idealist. Paul Theroux's definition of a cynic is a disappointed idealist. So as you go through past your twenties, your idealism is going to be disappointed many many times. And so, I've brought my view and also— I've just realized this—Libertarianism as I understood it was very good and pure and we're all going to be successful and generous to the less fortunate and it was, to me, not dark or cynical. But then I soon saw, of course, the way that it gets twisted by the flaws of humanity. And that's when I evolved now into ... a bleeding-heart Libertarian. That'll do.[46]

In his penetrating reflections on life, *Far and Away* (2011), he went into some detail about his beliefs, noting that one could easily call him a "quasi-libertarian (left-wing conservative, right-wing liberal, what have you)." In a catechesis, he writes:

Such reflections have led me to define myself in recent years as a "bleeding-heart libertarian."
Do I believe in the sanctity of the individual and all freedoms and rights?
Certainly.
Do I believe that humans should generously help others in need, and voluntarily contribute to public works of mutual benefit?
Why, yes, of course.
Do I believe that the general run of humanity can ascend to those noble heights of ... humanity?
Alas, I do not.
So ... lead left.[47]

In his excellent follow-up book, *Far and Near*, Peart explains this a bit further, in terms of freedom of immigration and gun ownership.

They were, I realized, memorials for people who had died trying to cross the desert to a new life in the United States. Sometimes groups of them were betrayed and stranded by their supposed guides, the "coyotes," to die in horrible ways. Sure, they were illegal aliens, or would-be undocumented workers, as you prefer, but—what to do? The great Western writer Edward Abbey's suggestion was to catch them, give them guns and ammunition, and send them back to fix the things that made them leave. But Edward Abbey was a conservative pragmatist, and I am a bleeding-heart libertarian—who also happens to be fond of Latin-Americans. The "libertarian" in me thinks people should be able to go where they want to go, and the "bleeding heart" doesn't want them to suffer needlessly.[48]

The term "bleeding-heart libertarian" has existed for only a decade or two. Most likely first coined by libertarian philosopher Roderick Long, Bleeding-Heart Libertarianism has found a large following among academics who oppose the stronger right-wing, conspiratorial elements present in more populist and political libertarianism. Among their number are very prominent American thinkers such as economist Steve Horwitz, literary critic Sarah Skwire, and political philosopher Matt Zwolinksi. All of them, interestingly enough, are also fans of Rush. Their motto is "Free Markets and Social Justice," believing that the real libertarian alliance should be with the civil libertarians of the so-called Left rather than with the anti-government elements of the so-called Right. Their counterpart within conservatism is the Front Porch Republicans who see a natural alliance between communitarians of all political backgrounds.[49]

Again, in his 2014 book, *Far and Near*, Peart explained his own understanding of politics: "Generally, while believing in individual rights and responsibilities, we favor the classic liberal values of generosity and tolerance, and fear the religious oppression that has wormed its way into modern Republican platforms. (And that is a good metaphor.)"[50]

Not surprisingly, given his own natural intelligence, his diligent scholarship, and his lifelong love of all things Rush, the person who best understands Peart's political views was Horwitz. In his definitive essay "Rush's Libertarianism Never Fit the Plan," Horwitz convincingly argued that whatever label Peart might give himself or others might give him, he remains impossible to categorize neatly. Peart, simply put, was too much of an individualist, always exploring, always growing in his own ideas. And not just Peart. "What we might call Rush's 'individualism' (and I do think this is a description that applies to all three band members)," Horwitz suggested, "provides the overarching philosophical theme of their career, from their own choices as a band to their lyrical content."[51]

To consider Peart a Randian and to stop there is beyond

unconscionable. It is, in the words of Peart, "lazy."[52] Peart certainly liked Rand, but he also read everything he could find and get his hands on as well. Truth to tell, Peart never stopped reading, and while Rand was an immense influence upon him when he was twenty-four, so were a vast number of other literary figures. Indeed, if Peart seemed to have found satisfaction with western philosophical teaching as culminating in the late eighteenth century, his literary tastes—which evolved over the past half century—remain mostly rooted in the period from Mark Twain to John Barth. Peart especially returned to the modernist writers of the post-World War I era. This is such a vital point to understanding Peart that it is worth quoting him at length:

I was always a great reader, and I was voracious through that time (ca. 1980). But I was reading as widely to John Dos Passos and John Steinbeck, Ernest Hemingway. A lot of American writers at the time, because I'd been through a lot of Charles Dickens and Thomas Hardy. Reading became not only my school room on the road but my sanity. People often ask me: when did you get tired of touring? The first month! It was like schlepping around like this when maybe you play 26 minutes that night but the rest of that time is just aimless—not only aimless but empty, unproductive time. You can't do anything except, I found, reading. And it was a way to fill those hours of waiting in a way that felt good. If nothing else you've got a book you've read at the end of that day. So I kind've poured myself into that in those days and read a ton of the English greats and then worked into the American greats, starting by that time. But, I can't say they were a huge influence on lyric writing per se. Because it's such a different craft. I always say the typical song has 200 words, you know, where a novel might have 40,000–50,000. So, you're dealing on a whole other canvas. Yes, I was learning from all of those writers about life and about the power of words, but I was kind've feeling my own way, craftwise. You know? Later on, I did start to explore more into poetics, especially when I was writing lyrics. I would be reading T.S. Eliot, or I would be reading

Robert Frost as a kind of exemplar of the highest that verse writing could be. And, of course, I was a lifelong music fan, so lyrics in general ... I already had certain preferences. I liked lyric words that made sense. I didn't like when they were too repetitive ... and I didn't like confessional sort of songs about people's hearts being broken by perfidious lovers and stuff.[53]

To catalogue the number of authors Peart admires would be a book in and of itself. In addition to the ones explicitly mentioned above, one could readily add Nathaniel Hawthorne, Herman Melville, Henry James, Wilkie Collins, Oscar Wilde, Virginia Woolf, Sinclair Lewis, Theodore Dreiser, Willa Cather, Edward Abbey, F. Scott Fitzgerald, Fritz Lieber, C.S. Lewis, Robert Pirsig, Wallace Stegner, Thomas Pynchon, John Barth, Tom Robbins, and Kevin J. Anderson to the list.[54] It is, yet again, worth quoting Peart at length:

Well, a lot of people don't pay attention to lyrics. As a listener, I don't. The only reason I put so much into writing is because I'm the one who's doing it. It's the old Anglo-Saxon ethic: if it's worth doing ...

Development? During Rush's early days my reading preferences—and they influence the way you write—were Victorian-era English literature: Thomas Hardy, Dickens; fantasies and science fiction—all of it written in a timeless, old-fashioned, ornate style. So my lyrics were all very ornamental. I'd take the germ of what I wanted to express and then dress it up, decorate it the way a Victorian house might be decorated, with all the gingerbread and fancy shutters.

Over the last couple of years my reading habits have followed the historical path of prose writing, and I've finally discovered the 20th century, the New World writers like Scott Fitzgerald, Hemingway, Faulkner, Barth—vigorous, economical writers who don't use adjectives for their own sake, but who succeed in saying in a single phrase what Hardy would have spent a couple of paragraphs on. Now, more and more, I'm trying to find some fundamental thing that can be expressed simply, where the choice of words is ultimately precise.... I've come to reflect on the exact meanings of words and word choices.

The rhythm, of course, reflects that simplicity. It's somewhat deceptive, because I spend a lot of time on it, but in the final analysis, it's some very simple thing. Hemingway wrote only 500 words a day, a very low output, but he agonized over his choice of words; his sentence construction was often illiterately simple—he'd eliminate so much, what was left would be almost unintelligible. I found that approach very useful in lyric writing.[55]

Rather humorously, Peart's mother confirms the same in the documentary film, *Beyond the Lighted Stage*. "He was ... in those days, I used to say 'weird.' ... He just read everything there was to read."[56] While many rock stars saw the touring life as one that would allow for decadence, hedonism, and self-absorption, Peart viewed it as a way toward true liberal education. "What more perfect portable education than having a lot of free time on your hands and bookstores everywhere," Peart said. "So, for the next few years, I started filling those years with reading."[57] In an interview in 1991, Peart put it succinctly: "There are so many books, so little time."[58]

During tours, Peart voraciously read three to four books a week.[59] He had no idea what might have happened to him with so much free time, all of it unproductive, had he not found books and other diversions.

I can divide my touring life into two phases, because I realized on the very first tour in 1974 that this was no kind of life, and there was so much hanging out time and it was potentially so self-destructive. And I started reading then, I filled all the empty hours with the education that I missed, delving into all the genres. There was the book period, and then in my thirties I got into bicycling and then into motorcycling, and they became the escape from touring and the injection of life, freedom, engagement with the world, and it's still something that I love.[60]

Not surprisingly, 2112 (released April 1, 1976) especially captivated the spirit of middle-American males in their teens and twenties. Suffering through defeat in Vietnam (and elsewhere), cowering to the Soviets, surviving Watergate with nothing more than intense cynicism toward all politics, and limping along economically, middle Americans decided to recapture the "Spirit of '76" and celebrate the two hundred years since the passage of the Declaration of Independence. In that spirit of patriotic defiance, the citizen became greater than the politician, the local community more vital than the behemoth on the Potomac.

Though the protagonist of 2112 ends his own life, in classical and Stoic fashion, he also won by denying the collectivist society from wielding any further control over his destiny. One of the most cherished myths of the American founding era was the true story of Cato the Younger who fought against Julius Caesar's takeover of the republic. When the great Stoic Cato realized Caesar would defeat his forces, he took his own life, placing his trust in a Platonic dialog dealing with the immortality of the soul. No story held greater sway over George Washington, who had memorized the eighteenth-century play *Cato: A Tragedy* by Joseph Addison. He also had it performed upwards of seven times during the fateful winter at Valley Forge as a way to inspire his troops. The story of Cato is as American as it is western. Hatred of communism and conformism as well as a patriotic (not nationalist) love of America would cause young American males to sympathize with the protagonist of 2112. He rebelled in the name of goodness, and like Cato the Younger, he chose his own end, despite overwhelming odds.

Peart considered the story of 2112 as nothing more than a warning—not a prediction of what was to come but of what *might* come.

Well, things aren't all that bad now, but it's a logical progression from some of the things that are going on. All of the best science fiction is a warning. We want to let people know what's going on so they at least have a chance to change it.[61]

In a world of Pol Pots and the Khmer Rouge, Peart's vision was indeed happening at the time of the release of *2112*, just not yet in the so-called free world.

The shorter songs of side two—"A Passage to Bangkok," "The Twilight Zone," "Lessons," "Tears," and "Something for Nothing"—continue to reveal the excellence of Rush, but they could not, understandably, live up to their older and more developed brother on side one. "A Passage" deals, somewhat controversially, with the drug trade in much of the third world, especially in South America and Asia. A journey, it embraces mysticism and some former hippie elements, and it does so in a musically compelling way, with oriental guitar riffs and rich hooks. Though more fluid, "A Passage" does somewhat resemble Led Zeppelin's "Kashmir."

"The Twilight Zone" provides an homage to Rod Serling. Interestingly enough, their producer through 1982s *Signals*, Terry Brown, believes this to be Rush's best song.

"The Twilight Zone" is a little gem with a very strong lead guitar motif from Alex, Ged's verse vocals up in the stratosphere and then the chorus slipping into an eerie flanged vocal that is in the "zone." This is all held together by Neil's very concise, driving percussion closing with the airy guitar solo which makes this one of my favourite Rush tunes.[62]

"Lessons" is the most folk-oriented of the songs, a sort of hard progressive singer-songwriter tune discussing authority and one's acceptance of responsibilities. "Tears" sees Rush flirt with a pop ballad, and "Something for Nothing" returns to the classic Peart themes of persistence, duty, and integrity as first explored in "Anthem."

You don't get something for nothing
You can't have freedom for free
You won't get wise with the sleep still in your eyes
No matter what your dreams might be

No lyrics could have better ended the album *2112*. They summed up every real lesson to be learned from Rush in 1976. If the protagonist of side one took his own life, Peart called for his listeners to embrace their own lives, take charge, and pursue the best within each of them. As Geddy Lee stated at the time, "The solution is more or less that we would like to present the germ of an idea to stimulate someone into thinking of a solution. However," he continued, "'Something for Nothing,' on the second side, is sort of a wrap-up of how we feel. It's not specifically part of the concept, but many songs on side two relate to the general theme. As for *2112* (side one), we say only what could happen but hopefully will not happen, and leave it up to the intelligence of the listener."[63]

Certainly, for Rush, the album *2112* made their career. In their desire to go down with an explosive sound and fury, they changed the entire trajectory of their history and, in fact, given Rush's importance and longevity, the history of rock itself. With the success of *2112*, Rush attained the independence necessary—not worrying about money and corporate control—to pursue their own artistic dreams from 1976 through their last tour in 2015. Though *2112* might have ended the band as effectively as the song's protagonist ended, the band instead became the protagonists of "Something for Nothing."[64] No sleep remained in their eyes.

None of this should suggest acceptance by the media elite. Once again, they savaged Rush. As the *Washington Post* claimed:

There were occasional echoes of Led Zeppelin, both in bassist Geddy Lee's vocals and Alex Lifeson's guitar riffs, but it's impossible to cite other influences simply because Rush's music, amplified beyond the threshold of pain, is essentially characterless.

On September 29, 1976, Rush released *All the World's a Stage*, an immense live album, a monument to their triumph as a band. They considered it the close of the first chapter of their story. In Great Britain, Geoff Barton especially continued to praise the band. "Direct, hard-hitting and powerful to the Nth degree. Rush are probably the best undiscovered band in Britain at the moment," he enthused. "I strongly recommend you to check them out, now!"[65]

A FAREWELL TO KINGS

What followed, 1977's *A Farewell to Kings*, though, had far more in common with 1976's *2112* than it would with 1980's *Permanent Waves*. Not appearing on the market until September 1, 1977, *A Farewell to Kings* ended the new-album-every-six-months schedule Rush had followed thus far. A brilliant album in and of itself, *A Farewell to Kings* still belongs to Rush 2.1 as I have defined it. So does the follow-up album, *Hemispheres*. Certainly, Rush tried more new things—in terms of album structure, lyrical depth and storytelling, and musical complexity—than it had on the first several albums.

"We had written material that was a little beyond us, considering our level of musicianship at the time," Lee later admitted.[66] But the progress was in continuity, a major reform rather than a revolution.

"Our progress has always been sincere—not in an arrogant way, but for our own pleasure," Peart stated in 1982. "We've always incorporated music from people we liked, so it has made us stylistically schizoid."[67]

While there are no side-length tracks on *A Farewell to Kings*, the album revolves around its two major songs, "Xanadu" at 11 minutes in length and "Cygnus X-1" at almost 10½ minutes. Thematically, Peart continues to embrace both the fantastic—"Xanadu" based on the iconic romantic English poem, "Kubla Khan," by romantic Samuel Coleridge—and science fiction, "Cygnus X-1." At the time, Peart lauded fantasy writing in lyrics. "It's a way to put a message across without being oppressive."[68]

It would be impossible to describe how much of an influence the moody, mysterious "Xanadu" had on the rock world. Its ability to combine high, poetic art with rock influenced many rockers and listeners alike. One of the greatest living American guitarists, John Wesley, who has released a number of solo albums as well as having worked with prominent bands such as Porcupine Tree, admitted that after hearing *A Farewell to Kings* for the first time, he was "blown away," but "the track that captured me was 'Xanadu.' It was the first Rush track I tried to learn from beginning to end." Though he struggled for years to get the piece right, in hindsight, he notes that the song proved a "turning point for me as a player."[69] One can also hear the album's immense influence on the more progressive tracks written by the prog metal band, Dream Theater.

The opening track, "A Farewell to Kings," harkens back to "Bastille Day" as well as *2112* in its challenge to authority. Here, though, authority has lost. The king, a jester at best and a puppet at worst, sits on his throne, dangling limp as the world around him has been destroyed. He governs nothing but Eliot's *The Waste Land*. In the vision of Peart and album designer Hugh Syme, free men and women have simply said "Enough," thus anticipating the Velvet Revolution of 1989. Another ballad, "Closer to the Heart," offers an idyllic view of the world, embracing the gentle classical liberalism of a Thomas Jefferson or a Benjamin Franklin.

Based on the Frank Capra movie of the same name, "Cinderella Man" asks why the best cannot be considered charitable rather than manipulative or crazy. Ironically, though many critics have labeled Rush Objectivist because of Peart's interest in Rand, placing Capra's film as heroic and noble goes against the very heart of Rand's philosophy. In the song, Lee (who wrote the lyrics) still embraces individualism, but he does so in a way that would not be recognized as good in Galt's Gulch, the individualist utopian Rocky Mountain hideout in Rand's *Atlas Shrugged*. The lyricist-bassist (very rare for Rush) sounds much more like Catholic social activist and social justice warrior Dorothy Day than the Nietzschean heroine of *Atlas Shrugged*, Dagny Taggart. Continuing in the medieval and bardic vein of the opening song, "Madrigal" has a Yes-like quality in its ethereality.

HEMISPHERES

1978's *Hemispheres* is a sequel to and completion of *A Farewell to Kings* from the previous year. Rush produces yet again a sidelong epic, thus completing the story begun at the very end of *Farewell*, the story of "Cygnus X-1." Taken all together, the story of Cygnus X-1 takes nearly 29 minutes to tell, making it the longest story Rush had yet told or would tell until 2012's *Clockwork Angels*. The one competitor, at least in terms of time needed to tell the tale, would be the Fear cycle told over four songs. Still, each of the four Fear songs deals with a different state of mind and does not construct a coherent story in the way that the stories of Cygnus X-1 or *Clockwork Angels*' Owen Hardy have. Just as *2112* blatantly revealed Peart's anti-authoritarian side, "Cygnus X-1" and *Clockwork Angels* equally demonstrate, yet again, his love of the journey and the necessity of forging one's own path in life. Of course, the anti-authoritarian side and the free will side are two sides of the same coin. One rages, while the other considers.

All of these strands of Peart's thought come together whenever he enters upon the subject of God, Christianity, and religion.

To put it mildly, Peart had a difficult time with religion and religious matters—especially formalized religion—ever since childhood. Indeed, he never had any faith in a higher power, even as a little boy.[70] While he joked about the subject and his obsession with it frequently, his disgust with religion comes through his lyrics and, especially, his books. Here's a typical example, taken from his 2011 book, *Far and Away*:

Fun Fact: The theological default called Pascal's Wager is a pusillanimous theorem stating that it's "safer" to believe in God than not, because you have nothing to lose if you're right, and everything to lose if you're wrong. All I can say to that is "Man up, Pascal!"[71]

Not surprisingly, Nietzsche wrote something quite similar about Pascal, calling him the most representative "worm" of Christianity, the worst of Catholicism in *Beyond Good and Evil*. Pascal possessed, the German philosopher decried, a wounded and monstrous "intellectual consciousness."[72] As will be seen later in this work, Nietzsche exerted a serious influence on Peart. As a child, Peart even spray-painted "God is Dead" on his bedroom wall.[73]

In 2014's *Far and Near*, Peart, asked if he's a "faith-basher," was somewhat appalled at the notion that he might be.[74] Certainly, though, Peart saw a significant difference between his toleration of religion and his (dis)respect for those same religions (and their deluded followers):

Those who attribute spiritual power to geological formations, a humorless deity, or articles of clothing (think Catholic, Hasidic, Mormon, or Buddhist) are difficult to respect—not so much for their "magic," but for their vanity. As for tolerance and respect, we agree that tolerance is necessary—people can believe the crazy fecal matter of their choice—but we're not sure about respect. Fundamentalists of every stripe, and likewise conspiracy theorists, are pretty much impossible to respect, especially if they preach violence—pain to others, the real first deadly sin. In terms of my simple moral compass ... if the greatest evils to an individual are pain, fear, and worry, then it stands to reason that the worst things you can inflict on another human being are pain, fear, and worry.[75]

Again, in *Far and Near*, he detailed how many religious billboards, bumper stickers, and signs he had encountered in the United States, clearly amused by the notion, even if repulsed by many of the ideas presented. He certainly mocked the idea of "putting your hand in the hand of the Judeo-Christian skygod," placing the Holy Trinity on the level of Apollo and Zeus, simply nice superstitions of an immature race.[76]

Here is Peart at length on Paganism and Christianity and faith bashing, again from 2014:

It is ironic that a religion that has historically co-opted prehistoric festivals for their own purposes would insist that pagans are unable to celebrate Christmas. Of course, it was ours first. The idea of grafting Christian festivals onto existing celebrations dates back at least to the eighth century, when Charlemagne massacred thousands of pagan Saxons for resisting his ... "missionary zeal." It is also arrogant to suggest that without religion we have no reason to feel "goodwill toward men." It isn't fear of godly punishment or promise of heavenly reward that makes generosity feel good—it's simple humanity. Any undamaged individual knows how good it can feel to help others. I would love to avoid the taint of "faith-basher," as I have been called, but a further irony is that the most fanatical "Christians" today are the most vocal against the biblical example of, say, being good Samaritans. They would proudly (and loudly) deny even mercy to the less fortunate.[77]

However much one agrees or disagrees with Peart's specific take on the relationship of paganism to Christianity, two things must be noted. First, Peart identified here not as an atheist, but rather as a pagan. Second, factually and historically, he was correct. Since St. Paul first journeyed to Athens, the Catholic

Church has attempted to co-opt and baptize the pagan rather than destroy it. Peart viewed this historical move of the Catholic Church as regressive rather than progressive, though, an act of dishonesty, manipulation, and theft. Indeed, religion as a whole, Peart believed, stands against and retards real progress toward liberalism, properly understood, and toward human freedom. For some, though, faith has been a good, he reluctantly admitted. For many, "it's definitely a positive sort of reinforcement or a kind of solace and those are all good things."[78]

Hemispheres came into the world on October 29, 1978. Its opening track, "Cygnus X-1, Book 2: Hemispheres," the conclusion to the Cygnus story, reveals the tensions in Peart's own mind between order and chaos, plan and anti-plan. Divided into six parts, it considers Apollo as wisdom, Dionysus as love, and Cygnus (Peart in fictional form) as the Aristotelian mean and balance. Only by embracing the two extremes, Peart argues through the voice of Cygnus, representing the voice of art and will, could one transcend this Manichean division.

We can walk our road together
If our goals are all the same
We can run alone and free
If we pursue a different aim
Let the truth of love be lighted
Let the love of truth shine clear
Sensibility
Armed with sense and liberty
With the heart and mind united
In a single
Perfect
Sphere

The conflict—which rages in every human heart—can resolve not just in a cease fire and a truce, but in an actual rebirth of a new creation.

The story itself comes directly from Friedrich Nietzsche's book on music, *The Birth of Tragedy*, in which he complained that our ordered society had become too complacent in matters of art and creativity:[79]

We shall have gained much for the science of aesthetics when we have succeeded in perceiving directly, and not only through logical reasoning, that art derives its continuous development from the duality of the Apolline and Dionysiac; just as the reproduction of species depends on the duality of the sexes, with its constant conflicts and only periodically intervening reconciliations. These terms are borrowed from the Greeks, who revealed the profound mysteries of their artistic doctrines to the discerning mind, not in concepts but in the vividly clear forms of their deities. To the two gods of art, Apollo and Dionysus, we owe our recognition that in the Greek world there is a tremendous opposition, as regards both origins and aims, between the Apolline arts of the sculptor and the non-visual Dionysiac art of music. These two very different tendencies walk side by side, usually in violent opposition to one another, inciting one another to ever more powerful births, perpetuating the struggle of the opposition only apparently bridged by the word "art"; until, finally, by a metaphysical miracle of the Hellenic "will," the two seem to be coupled.[80]

In our desire for stability, Nietzsche lamented, we lost the will to create, to innovate, and to steal fire from the gods. In his own later reflections on his treatise on aesthetics, the German philosopher chided himself for being too dualistic (too Hegelian) in his formulation of art. He attempted to round this out by claiming that Christianity represented a new way of thinking, neither Apolline nor Dionysiac. Instead, thinking even worse of it than he had in his previous work, Christianity actually negates all beauty. While the Greeks affirmed, the Christians offered nothing but nihilism in their oppression of the human spirit.[81] Though Peart did not reference Nietzsche often, when he did, he did so with approval or at least intense interest.

Elevating the conversation a little, I wrote down the day's church sign, saying it aloud to Michael, "Conquer Yourself, Rather Than the World."

Michael and I agreed that we would prefer a more Nietzschean interpretation: "Conquer yourself, then the world."[82]

In a short autobiography for a Canadian newspaper in 1994, Peart described his life through Nietzsche's famous motto: "That which does not kill me makes me stronger."[83] Throughout his adult life, Peart had taken Nietzsche rather seriously. After an interview in 2010, one Toronto journalist explained: "He not only longs for diversity, he speeds himself head-long into whatever project he chooses, be it reading Nietzsche, writing books, organizing tributes to jazz legend Buddy Rich or cycling across Africa."[84] Even a 2008 *Rolling Stone* article conceded that Peart's life is in and of itself a "Nietzschean creation story."[85] *Rolling Stone* had never been so correct in its judgment of Rush or of Peart.

Side one of *Hemispheres*, though musically very complex, had much more in common with previous Rush songs and albums than its second side did. Side two anticipated the next albums, *Permanent Waves* and *Moving Pictures*, serving, albeit only in hindsight, as a great transition. The first of the three songs on side two, "Circumstances," is only a little over 3½ minutes in length. Concisely and cleverly, the song tells the story of a boy trapped in his room, burdened by the weight of reality, only to realize his imagination can take him anywhere. While the song is quite good, "The Analog Kid," only a few albums away, would offer a much more driving and sophisticated look at the same theme.

"The Trees," track two on side two, has served as a divisive point for Rush fans since 1978. Those oriented toward libertarianism see the song as a rallying cry against the excesses and artificialities of imposed equality, while Rush's more philosophically moderate and left-leaning fans see it as nothing more than a story based on the cartoon that inspired the song in the first place. As Peart explained:

Lyrically that's a piece of doggerel. I certainly wouldn't be proud of the writing skill of that. What I would be proud of in that is taking a pure idea and creating an image for it. I was very proud of what I achieved in that sense. Although on the skill side of it, it's zero. I wrote "Trees" in about five minutes. It's simple rhyming and phrasing, but it illustrates a point so clearly. I wish I could do that all the time.[86]

When the maples believe the oaks—taller and sturdier—have taken all of the sunlight, they cry foul!

So the maples formed a union
And demanded equal rights
"The oaks are just too greedy
We will make them give us light"
Now there's no more oak oppression
For they passed a noble law
And the trees are all kept equal
By hatchet, axe and saw

While the song, so beautifully written, might serve as an allegory for many things, Peart's already professed and adamant individualism shaped the interpretation fans and critics have placed on the song. Certainly, in an age of holocaust camps, gulags, and killing fields, the support of the new law by its own terrors might have justly allowed the libertarian fans to treat this as yet another Rush anthem against the ever-devouring Leviathan of the State. That Lee scream-sighs the final line, "by hatchet, axe, and saw," seems to suggest French Revolutionaries, the KGB, or the Gestapo might well be involved in forced pogroms and collectivization schemes.

The final track, "La Villa Strangiato (An Exercise in Self-

Indulgence)," finds the band at its most humorous and at its brilliant best. At a little over 9½ minutes and absent any lyrics, this instrumental serves as the perfect ending to Rush 2.1. Even part 12 of the 12-part song is, appropriately, entitled, "A Farewell to Things." Though probably nothing more than a coincidence, it does so as a very telling one. It and "The Trees" have remained live fan favorites through to the present day. One of the greatest living drummers, Mike Portnoy, described rather gloriously why this song has meant so much to so many.

If I had to pick the quintessential Rush song, it would have to be "La Villa Strangiato." When I was a teenager in the early '80s and in the heat of my deepest Rush influence, that was the benchmark for instrumental prowess. Not only for us drummers, but also for fellow bass players—that quick bass and drum breakdown—and guitarists— perhaps still Alex Lifeson's greatest recorded solo. As I also stated in the Beyond the Lighted Stage *film, to us blossoming musicians at the time, [it] was the ultimate musical challenge to learn, as no other instrumental song in rock history had that level of technical precision.*[87]

Whatever Mike Portnoy thinks of the album now, at the time, critics had a field day attacking it. Longtime Rush stalwart, Geoff Barton, remained divided on the album (nothing to do with the album's main theme!):

Those are the basic essentials, anyway. But like I say, I'm really unable to decide whether Hemispheres *is a masterwork or a mistake. Sometimes the album sounds totally convincing; on other occasions it appears messy and disjointed, and yet I suppose the very fact that I'm uncertain about the merits of this LP makes it a failure. After all, in the past just about every Rush review I've written has brimmed over with superlatives ... and this time around you'd be hard pressed to find even one. When it comes down to it, I'd much rather hear about a battle between By-Tor and the Snow Dog than gods by the names of Apollo and Dionysus. Which would suggest that I reckon Rush should return to "basics" ... that they have become too ambitious for their own good.*[88]

Rolling Stone, however, offered an unusually kind review of the album.

Lifeson, Peart and Lee prove themselves masters of every power-trio convention. In fact, these guys have the chops and drive to break out of the largely artificial bounds of the format, and they constantly threaten to do so but never quite manage. If they don't succeed soon, complacency may set in. Already the lyrics are approaching a singsong regularity of meter, and the melodies are beginning to lean too heavily on mere chording. I affirm this band's ability to rock out, but I really want to give Rush a hard shove in the direction it's already heading.[89]

However one evaluates the album, on its own merits, it certainly signaled the end of Rush 2.1. Though remaining true to progressivism, the band would follow no preconceived ideas of what that might mean. "During *Hemispheres* we were like these monks," Lee remembered. "At one point during the album we stopped shaving, we sort of turned into these f---ing grotesque prog creatures in this farmhouse making the record, working all night, sleeping all day. *Permanent Waves* was quite the opposite."[90]

---

1. "Mystic Rhythms: Rush's Neil Peart on the First Rock Drummer," *NPR Morning Edition*, January 6, 2015.
2. Betsy Powell, "Peart is a Different Drummer," *Toronto Star* (June 30, 1997), pg. E4.
3. Peart, *Far and Near*, 6.
4. Dan Near, "Rush: Up Close," *Media America Radio* (January–February 1994).
5. Peart quoted in *Beyond the Lighted Stage*.
6. Peart quoted in Rex Rutkoski, "Interview: Neil Peart," *Rochester Freetime* (April 27–May 11, 1994).
7. Peter Howell, "Gold is the Color of Rush's Metal," *Toronto Sun* (October 19, 1993), C1.

8. Peart quoted in *Beyond the Lighted Stage*.
9. Dave Everley, "New World Man," *Prog* (February 2016): 55.
10. Geddy Lee quoted in *Beyond the Lighted Stage*.
11. Lee in Menon, *Rush: An Oral History Uncensored* (Star Dispatches, ibooks, 2013), no page numbers.
12. Lee quoted in Menon, *Rush: An Oral History Uncensored*.
13. Lifeson quoted in Menon, *Rush: An Oral History Uncensored*.
14. During the 2015 R40 tour, Rush finished the final four songs of the concert as though playing in the basketball gym of Rod Serling High School.
15. T.S. Eliot, *On Poetry and Poets* (New York: Farrar, Straus and Giroux, 2009), 21.
16. Geoff Barton, "Caress of Steel Review," *Sounds* (January 3, 1976).
17. I'm indebted to Steve Horwitz for pointing out the similarity between Lifeson's guitar work on *Caress of Steel* and Steve Hackett's work with Genesis at the same time. As usual, Horwitz was right.
18. David Brown, "Caress of Steel," *Record Mirror* (February 12, 1977).
19. Hamilton Place Official Program, February 9, 1976.
20. Neil Peart, "Life without the Possibility of Parole," in Stephen Humphries, *Art of Rush: Hugh Syme, Serving a Life Sentence* (2112 Books, 2015). This gorgeous book has no page numbers. Peart's piece is at the beginning of it.
21. One only has to look at the cover of *Grace Under Pressure* (1984), for example, to see every aspect of Syme's talent. True to the lyrical and musical content, the cover presents a deceptively calm scene. An android looks across an ocean toward mountains. Nothing is what it seems though. The water, calm upon first inspection is drifting in chaotic fashion off of the page, and the mountains in the distance reluctantly reveal the eye of a predator. Where the water meets the mountains, a mathematical expression is stamped: p/g. *Grace Under Pressure*. There should be no small amount of wonder when one considers that the art, the music, and the lyrics of this album inspired the first novel by Kevin J. Anderson, his excellent and chilling *Resurrection, Inc.*
22. Peart, *Roadshow*, 13.
23. Geddy Lee quoted in *Beyond the Lighted Stage*. See also Philip Wilding, "We Have Assumed Control," *Prog* (February 2016), 47.
24. Lifeson quoted in Menon, *Rush: An Oral History Uncensored*.
25. Peart in Dave Dickson, "Spirit of Peart," *Kerrang!* 44 (June 17–30/July 1–13, 1983). He also rejects the notion he is an "ist" of any kind except for an individualist. See, Peart quoted in Nicholas Jennings, "Rock N Roll Royalty," *Maclean's* (September 30, 1991).
26. Peart quoted in "Innerview with Neil Peart," Innerview with Jim Ladd (1984).
27. "Interview with Neil Peart," *Toronto Star* (September 9, 1993).
28. "Interview: Neil Peart," *Modern Drummer* (April 1984).
29. Peart quoted in Rick Johnson, *Creem* (March 1976).
30. "Rush: Time Traveling with Alex Lifeson: Conversation Conducted March 5, 2014," *Red Hot Rock* (May 2014), 15.
31. Peart quoted in Scott Bullock, "Neil Peart: A Rebel and a Drummer," *Liberty* (September 1997).
32. Budofsky, *Modern Drummer Legends: Rush's Neil Peart*, 23.

33. Budofsky, *Modern Drummer Legends: Rush's Neil Peart*, 23.
34. Nick Shofar, *Northeast Ohio Scene* (June 3, 1976); and Chris Welch and Brian Harrigan, "The Great Musicians: Neil Peart," *History of Rock* 10 (January 1984).
35. Scott Cohen, "The Rush Tapes, Part 1: Neil Peart Sizes Up 'Farewell To Kings,' The Latest Canadian Rock Opus," *Circus*, October 13, 1977).
36. Jon Pareles, review of *Exit ... Stage Left*, *Rolling Stone* (February 2, 1982).
37. Peart interview, *2112/Moving Pictures* Blu-Ray. First encountering the work of Samuel R. Delany in 1971, Peart found that science fiction was a genre of ideas and endless possibilities. This would play out in his own lyrics, but especially in this Clockwork trilogy, coauthored by Kevin J. Anderson.
38. Peart, *Traveling Music*, 218.
39. Peart quoted in Roy McGregor, "To Hell with Bob Dylan—Meet Rush. They're in it for the Money," *MacLean's* (January 23, 1978).
40. Peart quoted in Scott Bullock, "Neil Peart: A Rebel and a Drummer," *Liberty* (September 1997).
41. Norman Provencher, "Rush Rocks Right into the Order of Canada," *Ottawa Citizen* (February 26, 1997), B7.
42. Peart, "Hold Your Fire," *Backstage Club Newsletter* (January 1988).
43. Lee quoted in Stutz Fretman, "On the Art of Being Rush," *Hijinx* (January 1992).
44. Peart, "Counterparts," *Rush Backstage Club Newsletter* (January 1994); and Frank Lancaster, "It's True: The NMS Interviews Neil Peart," *National Midnight Star* (April 23, 1992).
45. Peart quoted in Scott Bullock, "Neil Peart: A Rebel and a Drummer," *Liberty* (September 1997).
46. Andy Greene, "Q&A: Neil Peart on Rush's New LP," *Rolling Stone* (June 12, 2012).
47. Peart, *Far and Away*, 261.
48. Peart, *Far and Near*, 58.
49. The fullest definition and understanding of "Bleeding-Heart Libertarianism" is at: bleedingheartlibertarians.com/ (now, sadly, defunct). The website defines those who advocate Bleeding Heart Libertarianism: "we are libertarians who believe that addressing the needs of the economically vulnerable by remedying injustice, engaging in benevolence, fostering mutual aid, and encouraging the flourishing of free markets is both practically and morally important. The libertarian tradition is home to multiple figures and texts modeling commitment both to individual liberty and to consistent concern for the marginalized, both here and abroad. We seek here to revive, energize, and extend that tradition—to demonstrate that contemporary libertarians can, in addition to their traditional vindication of individual liberty, offer effective, powerful, and innovative responses to the problems of economic vulnerability and injustice and to their social, political, and cultural consequences." In response, see Jeff Deist's "Neil Peart's Bleeding Heart," Mises Wire (October 1, 2018), mises.org/wire/neil-pearts-bleeding-heart.
50. Peart, *Far and Near*, 153.

51. Horwitz, "Rush's Libertarianism Never Fit the Plan," in Jim Berti and Durrell Bowman, eds., *Rush and Philosophy* (Chicago, IL: Open Court, 2011), 270.
52. Peart quoted in Mary Turner, "Neil Peart," *Off the Record* (August 27, 1984). In a 1992 interview, he claimed that he had not forsaken the ideas of Rand as much as he had moved well beyond her by reading so much more. See "It's True: The NMS Interviews Neil Peart," *National Midnight Star* (April 23, 1992).
53. Neil Peart interview, *2112/Moving Pictures* Blu-Ray.
54. It would be nearly impossible to cite every place Peart has mentioned a beloved and influential author. For a start, see Bruce Pollock, "The Songwriting Interview: Neil Peart," *Guitar for the Practicing Musician* (October 1986). See also, Paul A. Harris, "Lesson in How to Avoid Pitfalls of Rock n Roll," *St. Louis Post-Dispatch* (October 31, 1991); "Neil Peart on Rockline," Bob Coburn on Rockline (December 2, 1991); "Far and Near: An Interview with Neil Peart," *Huffington Post* (October 9, 2014).
55. Greg Quill, "New World Man," *Music Express* (September/October 1982). As mentioned at the beginning of this work, Peart and Kevin J. Anderson formed not only a close friendship, but they also became a dynamic writing team. In his discussion with the *Huffington Post* (October 9, 2014), Peart noted that Anderson serves as a "test reader," a confidante.
56. Neil Peart's mom quoted in *Beyond the Lighted Stage*. In the same documentary, Lee says something similar. Peart "was one of the weirdest people we'd ever met. Just because we didn't know anyone who was so literate and opinionated."
57. Neil Peart quoted in *Beyond the Lighted Stage*.
58. "Neil Peart on Rockline," Bob Coburn on *Rockline* (December 2, 1991).
59. Greg Quill, "Neil Peart: New World Man," *Music Express* (September/October 1982).
60. Peart quoted in Matt Scannell, "New World Man," *Prog* 52 (March 1, 2015), 35–36.
61. Peart quoted in Rick Johnson, *Creem* (March 1976).
62. Terry Brown, quoted in Malcom Dome, "Rush: R40," *Prog* 52 (January 2015): 41.
63. Nick Shofar, "Rush's 'Concept' is Rock and Roll," *Northwest Ohio Scene*, June 3, 1976.
64. Larry Rohter, "A Heavy Metal Juggernaut," *Washington Post* (April 19, 1977).
65. Geoff Barton, review of *All the World's a Stage*, *Sounds* (November 1976).
66. Geddy Lee quoted in *Beyond the Lighted Stage*.
67. Steve Morse, "Sending New Signals, Rush on the Defense," *Boston Globe* (December 6, 1982).
68. Graham Hicks, "Hemispheres: Shattered by Latest Rush Opus," *Music Express* (December 1978).
69. John Wesley, quoted in Malcolm Dome, "Rush: R40," *Prog* 52 (January 2015): 42.
70. Interview with Neil Peart, Jim Ladd, *Deep Tracks* (February 3, 2015).
71. Peart, *Far and Away*, 72.

72. Nietzsche, *Beyond Good and Evil: Prelude to a Philosophy of the Future* (New York: Vintage, 1989), 59.
73. Interview with Neil Peart, Jim Ladd, *Deep Tracks* (February 3, 2015). Peart explains the story in great detail, including the reactions of his mother and father, in travelogue of West Africa: *The Masked Rider* (1996; Toronto, ONT: ECW Press, 2004), 102.
74. Peart, *Far and Near*, 18–19.
75. Peart, *Far and Away*, 282.
76. Peart, *Far and Near*, 77. It should be noted that scholar Camille Paglia has described the Christian God in exactly the same manner.
77. Peart, *Far and Near*, 80.
78. "The Big Fresh," *Edmonton Journal* (December 3, 2006), B3.
79. Ula Gehret, "To Be Totally Obsessed—That's the Only Way," *Aquarian Weekly* (March 9, 1994).
80. Friedrich Nietzsche, *The Birth of Tragedy* (London, ENG: Penguin, 1993).
81. Friedrich Nietzsche, *Ecce Homo* (London, ENG: Penguin, 2004), 48–49.
82. Peart, *Roadshow*, 144.
83. Neil Peart, "A Port Boy's Story," *St. Catharines Standard* (June 24–25, 1994).
84. Alan Maki, "Peart Drums Up a New Hockey Theme," *Toronto Globe and Mail* (January 10, 2010).
85. Chris Norris, "Rush Never Sleeps," *Rolling Stone* (July 10–24, 2008).
86. Budofsky, *Modern Drummer Legends: Rush's Neil Peart*, 6.
87. Mike Portnoy, quoted in Malcom Dome, "Rush: R40," *Prog* 52 (January 2015): 44.
88. Geoff Barton, "It Could be a Meisterwerk," *Sounds* (October 21, 1978).
89. Michael Bloom, *Hemispheres* (Not Rated), *Rolling Stone* (March 22, 1979).
90. Philip Wilding, "On the Crest of a Wave," Classic Rock (May 2020): 27.

2 A NIGHT IN ZION
1980–1982

P*ermanent Waves* **(released January** 1, 1980) found the American public embracing Rush as never before. The first track, "The Spirit of Radio," opens with a soaring guitar riff so precise and so cleanly produced that it makes the band sound as though giving us their very first effort. Though some questioned the direction of their music away from long epics and traditional progressive rock structures, Rush's progressivism was truly progressive.

Living up to the true meaning of the oft-maligned word "progressive," we have consciously tried to get better—on our instruments, and in our songwriting, arranging, and performing. However, we have learned that such a path is never linear.[1]

And, in a very Peartian way, the song exudes warmth while also offering a philosophic meditation on excellence.

Invisible airwaves crackle with life
Bright antennae bristle with the energy
Emotional feedback on a timeless wavelength
Bearing a gift beyond price, almost free

All this machinery making modern music
Can still be open hearted
Not so coldly charted
It's really just a question of your honesty, yeah
Your honesty
One likes to believe in the freedom of music
But glittering prizes and endless compromises
Shatter the illusion of integrity

"Spirit of Radio" is nothing if not a refined explosion of energy. As progressive as anything Rush made before, the song offers a compact version of progression, even throwing in bits of Simon and Garfunkel as well as reggae. What would have taken ten minutes in Rush 2.1 takes only five minutes in Rush 2.2.

One of the most prominent musicians in progressive rock today, Andy Tillison of the English band, The Tangent, offers the best analysis of the song: "The song that drew me in the most was 'The Spirit of Radio.' This song hits me on a few levels lyrically, the most simple of which is my love of radio itself." For Tillison, the song succeeds on every level. "Lifeson's guitar at the beginning of the song with its delicate swirling phasing effect and sparkling pattern is a perfect prelude to the opening Peart-salvo 'Begin the day with a friendly voice.'" As a professor of music technology, this English progger believes the song demands one imagine Peart as a boy, discovering the world. "The line that suddenly pokes out of the song 'All this machinery making modern music can still be open hearted' was an affirmation of everything I wanted to do in life," he continues. The song in its lyrics and music bridged the old and the new, allowing one to flow from the other without erasing the past. "As I have written my own music over the past 35 years, that 'permission granted,' that manifesto or ideal has never been far from my mind. That electronic technology, like all other technologies as far back as the technology of language itself, will be best served up by the human element that can drive the machine." Ultimately, Tillison claims, the song demands the free will and agency of the artist over the material of her or his art. "The lines that follow are equally important, the fact that at root level it's really 'Just a question of your honesty' is another encouragement to the artist to spread his/her wings in the new technological backdrop—and the line 'Glittering prizes and endless compromises shatter the illusion of integrity, yeah!'—well this line is so beautifully cautionary, whether it's aimed at the Grammys, the weekly music charts, or the egocentric DJs at the hub of the celebrity culture of the '70s—the era of the song itself." That Peart understood all of this when so young astounds Tillison.[2] In every way, the track sees Rush embracing an important role, the soul of rock, in the 1980s.

Designed by Hugh Syme, the cover of *Permanent Waves* reveals a disastrous mess of sorts as a beautiful Donna Reed-like woman walks in the middle of it with Stoic confidence. She is, Peart admitted later, symbolic of the band. Through the popular fades of disco, reggae, and punk, Rush would chart their own course, doing so while embracing transcendent ideals. "That cover picture signifies," he said, "forging on regardless, being completely uninvolved with all the chaos and ridiculous nonsense that's going on around us." While any Rush fan could have claimed this already about the band, it is good to see the band confidently admit as much. Additionally, "she represents the spirit of music and the spirit of radio, a symbol of perfect integrity and truth and beauty."[3]

Socrates could not have stated it better.

In the second track, "Freewill," Peart again harkens back to his vital themes of individualism, perseverance, and acceptance of one's failures and successes. Just as crisp as "Spirit of Radio," but more direct in its straight-forward rock-and-roll hooks and riffs, Lee sings with absolute conviction the band's dedication to fighting the fates, never accepting second best.

You can choose a ready guide in some celestial voice
If you choose not to decide, you still have made a choice
You can choose from phantom fears and kindness that can kill
I will choose a path that's clear
I will choose free will

Few things angered or intrigued Peart as much as religion does, as noted in chapter one. It is a source of constant intrigue and constant frustration for him. As a libertarian, he naturally distrusted all authority, but he especially distrusted religious authorities.

Yet, while denying religious authorities any due, he did offer a "spiritual side" to his own beliefs. Following the theories of the Freudian psychologist and philosopher, Carl Jung, he noted: "I'm conscious of the gray zone between conscious and unconscious." These connections, however, are not religious. "A lot of my songs talk about that moment between sleep and waking," he continued. "If there is a spirit and soul in between the conscious and unconscious, mysterious connections come about." As with all things in this world, Peart hoped to analyze and incorporate such aspects of his being rather than allow them to dominate him and control his actions.[4] When pushed on the subject in 1994, Peart provided a classically Stoic response to faith.

Peart says he still employs considerable Biblical imagery in his lyrics "which I picked up as a child. I just encouraged my daughter to sign up for 'world religions' in high school. You should know those things. It is some people's solution to a problem."

Peart's background is Protestant. He implies that he no longer is involved with organized religion. "If there is life after death, I'm prepared for it," he says. "I think I've lived a good, responsible, moral life. But at the same time, only in service of my own idea of that. I think we are self-contained units of life and have to make the best of what we have here. Your job is to live a good life here and now. I hate the excuse 'it doesn't matter what your actions are here.' Spirituality is often a way of problem solving for people. They have needs or questions they can't answer and they accept religion to help them."

The source of creativity for Peart, one of rock's most intriguing lyricists, is excitement. "I get excited about things. The joy of creation is a small little spark," he says. "Suddenly you realize it's going to work. That's the joy you get—that it's going to work. Then you have to make it work. That takes another few days of craft. The little spark gets me interested."[5]

Creativity is spiritual, though not in a religious sense, he claims.

When Peart spoke in such terms, it is impossible not to compare him with another genius of his generation, Steve Jobs. The two have much in common, at least in terms of individualism and relentless drive. In all things, whatever they might be (except for his choice of official biographer), Jobs pursued excellence. Despite his embrace of eastern mysticism, various aspects of Hinduism, and Zen from a young age, Jobs's god seems to have been whatever was perfect and creative in man. The creativity, though, the founder of Apple thought, could only be presented by and through the agency of particular men and women. The source of excellence and beauty, however, came from beyond. Tellingly, after Yo-Yo Ma performed privately for him in his own home, Jobs wept (he cried all of the time, it should be noted; he never hid any emotion, good or bad). "Your playing is the best argument I've ever heard for the existence of God, because I don't really believe a human alone can do this." Whatever their differences in actual theology, Jobs and Peart agreed on the genius of man, and each represented the highest form of individuality in the 1980s, pursuing excellence in all things.

More recently, "Faithless," from the 2007 album, *Snakes and*

Arrows, serves as a sort of coda to 1980's "Freewill." "That's so long ago," Peart stated in a 2007 interview, and "so much has happened to me in the meantime. And yet the basic simplicity of what I thought then is true."[6] He had, he argued, gotten along rather well in life without the need for faith.

Paradoxically, the final track of side one of *Permanent Waves*, "Jacob's Ladder," embraces a deeply religious—specifically Old Testament—theme, the interplay of nature and the divine as the patriarch Jacob dreams of a stairway to the gates of Heaven. In Jewish as well as Christian theology, a question remains as to just what the ladder is. That is, what allows Jacob to ascend? By far the most musically progressive of the tracks on the first side, "Jacob's Ladder" employs martial beats and rhythms as it explores the godlike clash of weather systems and the dreams of men. "The clouds prepare for battle," the lyrics run, a play not just on nature but on man challenging the power of the gods as well. As Hebraic as "Jacob's Ladder" might be, it is also Promethean. As nature rages, man sees through its cracks. "Follow men's eyes as they look to the skies/The shifting shafts of shining weave the fabric of their dreams."

The first two tracks of side two, "Entre Nous" and "Different Strings," explore a more chamberlike form of rock, offering acoustic passages and singer/songwriter-like lyrics. In the way he sings Neil's lyrics, Geddy invites the listener into an intimate community of musicians and artists. "Who has come to slay the dragon?" the singer asks, quietly inviting the listener to take part in his own battles against his own personal demons.

Some songs just scream "let me reach perfection." Every note, every pause, every ebb, every swell, every silence, and every word just gravitates towards its right place. It's as though the cardinal and Platonic virtue of Justice—to give each thing its due—becomes manifest, real, and tangible in this world of shades, forms, and shadows. There probably are very few perfect tracks—tracks that never grow old and never cease to cause wonder. From the '70s and '80s, the following songs immediately spring to my mind as candidates: "The Battle of Evermore," "Spirit of Eden," "In Memory of Elizabeth Reed," "Close to the Edge," "In Your Eyes," "Thick as a Brick," "Cinema Show," "Echoes," and "The Killing Moon."

Of all of these great possibilities from those two wild and woolly decades, the one song that comes closest to attaining perfection, such as perfection is understood in this rather bent world, is "Natural Science," the final track on Rush's *Permanent Waves*.

Originally, as is well known by Rush fans, Peart had hoped to write a saga, epic, or edda about the Court of King Arthur and especially about the character of Sir Gawain.

I had also been working on making a song out of a medieval epic from King Arthur's time, called "Sir Gawain and the Green Knight." It was a real story written around the 14th century, and I was trying to transform it while retaining its original form and style. Eventually it came to seem too awkwardly out of place with the other material we were working on, so we decided to shelve that project for the time being....

With the departure of "Gawain" we had left ourselves nothing with which to replace him!

Something new began to take shape. It was the product of a whole host of unconnected experiences, books, images, thoughts, feelings, observations, and confirmed principles, that somehow took the form of "Natural Science" ... forged from some bits from "Gawain," some instrumental ideas that were still unused, and some parts newly written.[7]

Though he had decided against relying on science fiction as the sole way of telling stories, Peart still lingered in a bit of a myth/fantasy/Tolkien phase as he considered the lyrics for this song. Many of the ideas in "Natural Science," at least musically, also came from a "mass of ideas called Uncle Tounouse."[8]

At 9 minutes 17 seconds, "Natural Science" consists of three parts: "Tide Pools"; "Hyperspace"; and "Permanent Waves." These might have also have been titled, less poetically, Nature; Science; and Integrity.

In Part I, "Tide Pools," Peart offers a vision of community. Each person is born into a myriad of factors. As the great Irishman Edmund Burke once said before Parliament: "Dark and inscrutable are the ways in which we come into the world." Each person is born into a family, an environment, a language, a set of morality, and a religious system (even if atheist). Each of these factors shapes and delimits our very beings, and we must—from our earliest infancy—learn to move from one realm into another. We must transition, we must bridge, we must understand, and we must integrate our experiences. Such a world of communities brings us security, but it might also allow for an insular kind of inbreeding and sloth. Looking at all of the connections and interactions, though, overwhelms us.

Wheels within wheels in a spiral array
A pattern so grand and complex
Time after time we lose sight of the way
Our causes can't see their effects

Part II, "Hyperspace," reveals how dangerously insane an integrated, uniform culture might become. Peart's vision of conformity here is not of a communist or fascist variety, but instead of a capitalist, consumerist variety. It might metastasize uncontrollably.

A mechanized world out of hand
Computerized clinic
For superior cynics
Who dance to a synthetic band
In their own image
Their world is fashioned —
No wonder they don't understand

Part III, "Permanent Waves," brings the story and listener to a Stoic resignation, a realization that one must somehow and in some way recognize the limits as well as the advantages of an insular community and a hyper-collectivist consumerism, brought together by colossal bureaucracies of corporations, educational systems, and governments. The true man, whatever the odds against him, will survive.

The most endangered species
The honest man
Will still survive annihilation
Forming a world
State of integrity
Sensitive, open and strong

These are quintessentially Peartian themes, and he returned to them again and again in his lyrics. "Subdivisions," for example, offers almost all of the same sentiments, but it does so in lyrics that are much more direct and concise. The lyrics for "Natural Science" remain far more poetic than intellectual as well as far more artistic than philosophical. And yet, they are poetic, intellectual, artistic, and philosophical all at once.[9]

As always, reviewers offered mixed reviews of the album. "*Permanent Waves* will come as no great revelation to Rush fans, but should be recognized as a steady, definitive step in the band's evolution," Keith Sharp of *Music Express* wrote. He gave the album a 7 out of 10.[10] *Rolling Stone* even conceded, however grudgingly:

True, earlier LPs like Fly by Night *and* Caress of Steel *bear the scars of the group's naïveté. But now, within the scope of six short (for them) songs, Rush demonstrate a maturity that even their detractors may have to admire. On* Permanent Waves, *these guys appropriate the crippling riffs and sonic blasts of heavy metal, model their tortuous instrumental changes on Yes-style British art rock and fuse the two together with lyrics that—despite their occasional overreach—are still several refreshing steps above the moronic machismo and half-baked mysticism of many hard-rock airs.*[11]

Yet, true to *Rolling Stone* fashion, only a few months later, the magazine referred to Rush as "Heavy Metal Sludge," a teeny-bopper male fantasy band, equivalent to the then-heartthrob-musician and actor Shaun Cassidy. Cruelly, the review concluded:

For the record, those three are drummer Neil Peart, who writes all the band's lyrics and takes fewer solos than might be expected; guitarist Alex Lifeson, whose mile-a-minute buzzing is more numbing than exciting; and bassist, keyboardist and singer Geddy Lee, whose amazingly high-pitched wailing often sounds like Mr. Bill singing heavy metal. If only Mr. Sluggo had been on hand to give these guys a couple of good whacks.[12]

RPM Weekly praised the album for its innovation and its incorporation of currently popular trends in music.[13] *Melody Maker* offered the highest praise, noting that Rush could rest easy "in the knowledge they've once again scored a winner."[14]

MOVING PICTURES

Rush's next release, *Moving Pictures* (February 12, 1981), completes what *Permanent Waves* began, and the audience for Rush continued to grow by immense bounds. The iconic and perfect opening track, "Tom Sawyer," presents yet another anthem of individualism, the greatest Rush would produce.

No his mind is not for rent
To any god or government
Always hopeful, yet discontent
He knows changes aren't permanent
But change is

Much to the chagrin of the members of Rush, a number of American politicians—such as Senator Rand Paul of Kentucky—have adopted this song as their own personal anthem. Steve Rothery, the guitarist for the English progressive rock band, Marillion, understands the song's importance best. "Tom Sawyer is probably my favourite Rush track of all time. It has all the elements that make them such a great band. With a great groove, several hooky riffs and a strong and anthemic vocal. The *Moving Pictures* album is by far and away my favourite album of theirs. And this is the prime cut from it."[15] With lyrics co-written by fellow Canadian and friend, Pye Dubois, Peart's "Tom Sawyer" could be an autobiographically mythic statement. Certainly, it is the song most associated with Rush, seen equally as a statement of integrity and of arrogance. "Tom Sawyer" is probably the man most American males, at one time or another, would like to be. Peart's Tom Sawyer is freed from all restraint but still chooses to do the right thing, no matter the cost. Tom Sawyer, at least in the song, is a sort of modern demi-god, fully in control of his destiny, even when that destiny turns against him.

Inspired by a 1973 short story by Richard Foster, "Red Barchetta" is a science fiction dystopian short story, one that engages the themes of nostalgia, motion, speed, and defiance.[16] In Peart's version, the government has outlawed all personal transportation, but the protagonist takes his uncle's "brilliant red Barchetta, from a better vanished time" out into the country. There, he encounters a government vehicle of enforcement, "a gleaming alloy air car," and thus begins a deadly race. A second government vehicle joins the pursuit, but the hero breaks free, leaving the mobile leviathans at a bridge that cannot accommodate their girth. The song ends with the uncle and nephew, seated next to the hearth of home, dreaming of possibilities. For Peart, few stories could have tickled more of his fancies: the oppressive government, the fast car, the motion, the independence, and the color red.

After the hard-rock, jazz-tinged instrumental, "YYZ," the final track of side one is "Limelight." In nothing less than a confession, Peart describes exactly how uncomfortable he has become with fame and all of its trappings and demands. He cannot, he laments, "pretend a stranger is a long-awaited friend." To do so would reek of dishonesty, a trait Peart despises with all the force imaginable. And not surprisingly, friendship does not come easily to the drummer and lyricist, though his loyalties, when established, remain deep. Yet, he could not handle the obsession of fans who followed him off stage, to his hotel room, and even to his home. All of this behavior shocked him to no end. As he noted, he wanted to be good, not famous. He wanted recognition for his talents and hard work, not for his face. For most people, however, there is a very fine line between fame and excellence. "I love being appreciated. Being respected is awfully good. But anything beyond that just creeps me out," Peart says. "Any sense of adulation is just so wrong."[17] His discomfort with fame seemed to have grown as he aged.

Paradoxically, though Peart had put himself in the public eye for nearly five decades—in his music, his many books, and a nearly impossible number of interviews to count—he despised having his privacy and space invaded, having fans fawn over him, and having too much attention directed toward him. He wanted to be known for his skills, his insights, and his intelligence, but not for what brand of shoes he wore or what he did on a certain day with his beautiful wife and daughter. Praise brought him embarrassment and uneasiness.

"Neil has a real struggle with fans," Lee said. "It's not a personal thing, it's a shyness thing. He's not as able to be as relaxed around strangers as Alex or I am. He doesn't mean to hurt anyone's feelings by it. He's not trying to be rude."[18]

In a number of interviews, Peart tried to explain his reluctance to be famous. "I can't relate to people who have a one-sided view of me, thinking that they've known me for all these years and they know everything about me." Too many fans, he claimed, have gone berserk around him.[19] His anger stems not from arrogance about himself and his desire for privacy but from his own insecurities about being inadequate as a person.

And trying, the philosophy of Tryism, is the key to much about me, my attitude toward fans, other artists, and my own self-image. If I am uncomfortable with strangers making a fuss about me, and feel embarrassed by any show of admiration, people sometimes accuse me of thinking I am "too good." In fact the opposite is true—I don't believe I deserve that kind of attention. I have never thought I was very good at anything; I just tried hard. And nothing came easily. Having one's childhood personality shaped by being inept at every sport is a cliché, but it had its effect on me. What else do people judge you by at that age?"[20]

Further, he continued.

That sense of self affects my outlook in so many ways, rooted in the deep-seated belief that I am nothing special, and anyone could do what I do, if they only tried. It may not be true, but it is how I feel, and thus I don't overvalue what I do, or what I am. I hit things with sticks—big deal.[21]

Additionally, he resented the notion that he plays for his fans and their desires. This would be impossible, given the number of fans, but it would also diminish Peart's personal integrity and, consequently, his very appeal to them. "If you think that we have to please the fans that like Iron Maiden and Saxon and AC/DC—I know I have nothing in common with those people, so I can't possibly hope to be able to relate to them unless I play down or unless I talk down or think down."[22] For those who find his words inspirational, seeing him as a guru, Peart took neither credit nor blame. "I'm in no control of a thing like that." Does he like it? No. "But it's not something I can do anything about." Nobody, he stressed, had a right to him, or to any private aspect of him. He merely wanted to be a "normal human being."[23] Fans, he believed, "force us to protect ourselves. They force us to check into hotels under false names. They force us to have security guards to keep people away from us."[24] Peart remembered well the first time fans made him uncomfortable. He recounted this at length in his profound book, *Roadshow*, a travel memoir of Rush's thirtieth-anniversary tour:

Our popularity increased slowly, more or less gradually, but still eventually brought strange changes in the way people around us behaved. One afternoon, before a show at a small arena in the Midwest around the spring of 1976, three or four of us from the band and crew were on a lawn outside the venue, throwing a Frisbee around. Young long-haired males began gathering, just staring at us, apparently fascinated by our Frisbee-playing. We exchanged looks, but kept throwing and catching. Then some of the watchers started yelling out our names, and calling others over, until there were dozens of people around us. That kind of appreciation was what we were out on the road working for, of course, but not so much for our Frisbee-playing, and as the crowd grew bigger, the fun seemed to go out of the game.[25]

If things were uncomfortable for Peart in the 1970s, his discomfort increased exponentially with the success of 1981's

Moving Pictures and Rush's meteoric rise in the public eye in the early 1980s. Indeed, Peart remembered the entire year after its release with mixed emotions. "A lot of strange people came out of the woodwork" in the spring and summer of 1981, he recounted. "There was so much attention on us that was transitory."[26]

In his memoir of fourteen months on what he calls "The Healing Road," *Ghost Rider*, after the twin tragedies of the loss of his daughter and wife, Peart discovered something about his pre-1997 self:

In my former shallow, perhaps callous, world-view, I had enjoyed my life and appreciated my family and my friends, but I had often been annoyed by the feeling that everyone else just wanted something from me. But now life, which I had once idealized as a generous deity offering adventure and delight, had betrayed my faith viciously, and in the aftermath it was people who had held me up and held me together with unstinting care and unimagined affection.[27]

Of course, it was not just Peart who had problems with fans, though he was probably the most sensitive to the change in status and popularity. Lee and his family had to flee their home after fans stalked him in his neighborhood.[28] "I don't get tired of being in a band but I get tired of the name Rush," the bass player stated in 1982. "I get tired of being popular." He only wanted to be a great musician, not a star. "We've all gotten very protective," he said in an interview with a British magazine. "We value our privacy a lot and I think we've learnt how to put up a wall between ourselves and other people at times."[29] Peart joked that Rush "could start a 'Flake of the Week Club' based on some of its mail."

"Zealots who believe they've discovered the 'message' behind his words" especially frightened him.[30] Just what these hidden messages were are not clear. Presumably, Peart meant claims of aliens rather than claims of libertarian individualism.

Track four, "The Camera Eye," offers a John Dos Passosesque view of two cities, New York's Manhattan and London. The most traditionally progressive of the tracks on *Moving Pictures*, "The Camera Eye," at just under 11 minutes, remains the longest single Rush track from then until now.

Pavements may teem
With intense energy
But the city is calm
In this violent sea

Moody and introspective with punctuated energy, the music and lyrics offer an almost alienated and existentialist view of urban living. For all intents and purposes, it resembles "Natural Science" not just in length, but in themes as well. Here, in "The Camera Eye," the cities, rather than the tide pools, provide the locales vital to life. Yet, the individual walks through them in a bit of a daze, as the energy of so many urbanites combines, fuses, and overwhelms.

The second track on side two, "Witch Hunt," intrigued fans as Peart had mysteriously subtitled it "Part III of Fear." Only slowly did fans realize that Rush was releasing the first three parts in backward order, a new segment released on three successive albums. A four-plus minute version of the famous cautionary western American novel about the dangers of mobs, *The Oxbow Incident*, "Witch Hunt" warns against the group action of evangelicals driven by a false and overbearing sense of morality. Musically as well as lyrically, "Witch Hunt" is fraught with suffocation and claustrophobia, but it is also profoundly cinematic, as is every song on *Moving Pictures*.

The righteous rise
With burning eyes
Of hatred and ill-will
Madmen fed on fear and lies

To beat and burn and kill
Quick to judge
Quick to anger
Slow to understand
Ignorance and prejudice
And fear walk hand in hand ...

The final song, "Vital Signs," more new wave than anything else on the album, once again offers not only the perfect conclusion to this album but also a stunning segue to the next, 1982's *Signals*. In grand contrast to the narrowness of the mob in "Witch Hunt," "Vital Signs" opens a world of possibilities, especially for the creative individual: "Everybody got to elevate from the norm." The listener moves from tightness of breath to free and ecstatic inhalations and exhalations. Though written quickly, the song and especially its lyrics reflect Peart's well-considered theme that technology, rather than dominating human experience, might well mimic our human nature, thus remaining under our control. That is, Peart considers the possibility that the microchip works because it reflects our very human understanding of the natural order.

If Rush's clout and fanbase increased with *Permanent Waves*, it skyrocketed with *Moving Pictures*. This album not only became the iconic Rush album, it also became one of the all-time classics of album rock, rock, and progressive rock radio. *Sounds* declared after *Moving Pictures* appeared that Rush were "peerless," giving the album a perfect rating.[31] *Hit Parader*, however, got it best:

With the success of *Moving Pictures*, Rush stands on the verge of claiming recognition as one of the premier hard rock bands. They have finally conquered whatever musical stigmas that have plagued their career. By infusing new ideas into their metallic style Rush has become the spearhead of heavy-metal's creative evolution.[32]

Though *Rolling Stone* ignored the album, the fans did not.

Two months after *Moving Pictures* appeared, the RIAA certified it gold. Two weeks later, the album hit platinum. Fourteen years later, it had hit platinum four times, and, since, has gone platinum yet again.[33]

SIGNALS

The last album produced by the silent-fourth-member of Rush, Terry Brown, *Signals* (September 9, 1982) marked yet again a major progression in the music of Rush as well as in Neil Peart's lyrics. The pressure to produce something similar to the previous year's *Moving Pictures* naturally proved immense, as they had never encountered such success. On the *Moving Pictures* tour alone, fan attendance doubled at concerts, and almost anyone in the American Midwest could hear one of three tracks from the album almost anytime on FM rock radio. But the three main members of Rush decided that a second *Moving Pictures* would be too easy. They had done that album, accomplished what they had sought to accomplish, and they wanted to take their music in new directions. In particular, Lee had become more and more interested in keyboards and composing on them. He never planned to become a "Keith Emerson," but he appreciated the challenge the keyboards brought him.[34] Not surprisingly, especially given Lee's interest and the learning curve he needed to understand and overcome regarding synthesizers, the keys employed on the album had either 1) a deep, booming bass sound or 2) an airy, soaring feel. Lee remembers:

I was getting bored writing. I felt like we were falling into a pattern of how we were writing on bass, guitar and drums. Adding the keyboards was fascinating for me and I was learning more about writing music from a different angle.[35]

Further, he claims, the keyboards allowed Rush to expand beyond the power trio format without actually adding a new member of the band.[36] With *Signals* and the following concerts to support it, Lifeson claimed he felt "almost re-born" with the new sound.[37]

As each of the members of Rush have stated many times about themselves, they were sponges, soaking up the best in current music as well as the best in traditional literature. In particular, the band had been listening to the moody prog electronica of Ultravox and Japan, the moody pop electronica of Orchestral Manoeuvres in the Dark (OMD) and Spandau Ballet, and other synthesizer-driven and drowned-in-layers-of-sound new wave bands.[38] "Just as with many new wave groups, we have the same spirit of rebellion against mercenary forces," Peart stated in a phone interview.[39] The pre-concert mixed tapes that Peart created explain much:

The cassettes from the Signals tour, in 1982, neatly hand-labeled on the spine, "Rush Radio," and with my drawing of the fire hydrant logo from the album cover, offered a selection of lesser-known songs from that era, by New Musik, Simple Minds, King Crimson, U2, Ultravox, Max Webster, Joe Jackson, Japan, Thinkman, Go, XTC, Talking Heads, Jimmy Cliff, a couple of Pete Townshend's solo songs, Bill Bruford's jazz-rock excursions, and the ponderously-named-but-ethereal-sounding Orchestral Manoeuvres in the Dark.[40]

Given such diverse but intense influences, *Signals* was the darkest and moodiest album from Rush thus far, as dense as rock albums come. And some rock appearing at the same time appalled Peart. In one interview, he complained about his former hero, Carl Palmer, then playing for the so-called supergroup Asia. "I don't understand why any drummer would want to drop everything they learned like that and go back to kindergarten stuff."[41]

Lee had similar thoughts, though without naming names. "It all sounds the same now. At one point it all came charging back and had a lot of energy, but it hasn't really gone anywhere," the bassist explained. "It's just become a commercial thing, all pasteurized and homogenized. Anyone can pick up a book and learn a few heavy metal chords."[42]

From the ominous opening notes of "Subdivisions," the listener knows this is a Rush to be taken with deadly seriousness. No hobbits dwell here. There's a Tom Sawyer lurking somewhere in the neighborhood, but even he avoids such heaviness of mood as found on the first side of the album. Lots of honest men, however, populate *Signals*. All of this gravitas hovers over the entire album, despite the rather whimsical cover of a dog ready to mark his territory on the neighborhood fire hydrant. Only a few months after its release, Peart explained that the album had "more to do with writing about people and less about ideas. *Permanent Waves* was probably our first album that was in touch with reality—it was about people dealing with technology instead of people dealing with some futuristic fantasy world or using symbols for people. Now I'm trying to make those symbols into real people and real conflicts in real people's lives. I still want to write about ideals, I'm not interested in writing about the sewer of life."[43]

The album as a whole revolves around a song cycle. In 1982, immediately after the release of the album, an insightful interviewer said: "*Signals* has a cyclical framework. It opens in suburbia, on the edge of 'the far unlit unknown,' contemplates escape in 'The Analog Kid,' explores universal imponderables—the essence of our humanity, sex, religion, old age—and ends with actual escape to the stars in 'Countdown.'" Peart responded, presumably with a bit of surprise: "You noticed that. We were hoping no one would. It's so unfashionable these days to construct grand concepts. We're being closed mouthed about it. Some people, and I don't expect there will be many, will be insightful enough to catch it."[44]

The pounding synthesizer of "Subdivisions" introduces us to the alienated, creative individual, the one who fits into no groups.

Yeah, it's a common background for each of us, and I kind of think it's a background for a lot of our audience, too. For all its blandness, it's so easy to satirize, which is a trap I wanted to avoid. It's always been a constant stock joke or skit or something, to satirize the suburbs and mentality of it and all. And of course it's just as diverse as people are really, when you come down to it. But it has its own set of values and set of background parameters about it, which as you say are very much unique to this contemporary society.[45]

The protagonist is the one shunned by all of the "cool kids," those who through fortune or assertion consider themselves the "in crowd."

Growing up it all seems so one-sided
Opinions all provided
The future pre-decided
Detached and subdivided
In the mass production zone
Nowhere is the dreamer
Or the misfit so alone

In no other song does Peart so dramatically attack the foundations of modernity and its attempt to create false realities in the name of comfort and conformity. His critique rings true, harkening back to much of the cultural criticism of the post–World War II West. Peart's criticism, though concise, reflects the work of a number of the best cultural critics of the 1950s and 1960s, from C. Wright Mills to Thomas Merton to Russell Kirk to Jack Kerouac. In the mind of each of these critics, we conform to the patterns of corporate and corporatized society only at the cost of our individual souls.

Some will sell their dreams for small desires
Or lose the race to rats
Get caught in ticking traps

The second track, "The Analog Kid," a Bradbury-esque look at youth, imagines the vivid and imagistic dreams of a boy, a younger Tom Sawyer, yet to be jaded by the horrors of the world. As he innocently fantasizes about the first beautiful girl he's encountered, he

Lies in the grass, unmoving
Staring at the sky
His mother starts to call him
As a hawk goes soaring by
The boy pulls down his baseball cap
And covers up his eyes

If not a Tom Sawyer, at least a character straight out of the pages of *Dandelion Wine* or *Something Wicked This Way Comes*. Much of the story comes from Peart's own infatuation with a girl from Ohio he met, appropriately enough, during the Summer of Love: 1967.[46]

With "Chemistry," Peart shifts perspective, giving the listener a solid scientific look at the processes of the world, but with the protagonist of the previous song, wondering what connects A and B, C and D, and H and O. Surely, the song offers, in all of the chemical catalysts, collisions, and synergies, emotion and imagination play a role, connecting that tangible with the intangible. Interestingly enough, given the title, the credits attribute the lyrics to all three members of Rush. Lifeson and Lee told Peart what words they wanted in the song, and Peart put the final product together.[47]

"Digital Man," track four, considers the man of science, detached from the romance of nature, but longing for something greater than mere facts. He possesses a myriad of facts, but no connections to the highest things of life.

He'd love to spend the night in Zion
He's been a long while in Babylon

He'd like a lover's wings to fly on
To a tropic isle of Avalon

In the end, like everyone, he will exit this world, awaiting "a date in a black sedan." Until then, he will exist as a man who understands everything and, really, nothing. In the official *Signals Tour Book*, Peart explains that he had written the "The Analog Kid" as a companion piece to "Digital Man."

The first track of side two of *Signals*, "The Weapon," is the second part of the Fear Trilogy (actually a tetralogy, as *Vapor Trails* would eventually reveal). Beginning with a play on President Franklin Roosevelt's first inaugural speech during the Great Depression ("the only thing we have to fear is fear itself"), Peart again looks at the role of facts and the connections in story and mythology. We can, he notes, delude ourselves into believing we're safe under the iron fist of the state or the soft promises of religion or the plush and brightly colored toys of the corporate world. The real man, the man of integrity, is however

… not afraid of your judgment
He knows of horrors worse than your Hell
He's a little bit afraid of dying—
But he's a lot more afraid of your lying

Those in power jealously guard their ability to create and instill fear, as they know it is what allows them to rule. The song employs ska as well as something approaching "disco." "It's an all-out production number that we can play live, so I'm sure all the 'disco kids' will soon be coming to our concerts," Peart facetiously imagined. "Ha!"[48]

A song written at the last moment by the band, "New World Man" (a.k.a. "Project 3:57"), is exactly what the title claims, a consideration of the man of America. Here we have James Fenimore Cooper's great frontier hero of New York, Natty Bumppo, or perhaps John Wayne's Ethan Edwards (John Ford's *The*

Searchers) ready to face challenges, ready to become better, ready to become fully human.

He's a rebel and a runner
He's a signal turning green
He's a restless young romantic
Wants to run the big machine

As long as he learns from his mistakes, he will prosper.

Still, as "Losing It" reveals, one might very well fail to live up to one's own potential. This might result from giving too much too soon, or from failing to live by one's honesty, or by giving into one's self-reservations. The song, in large part, is an homage to Hemingway and his tragic end.[49] Would it be worse to have never tried or to have tried and failed? "For you—the blind who once could see—the bell tolls for thee."

Ending on the most upbeat note possible, the final song, "Countdown," narrates the historical launch of the NASA space shuttle *Columbia*. It is a paean to the explorers of the unknown and to the scientists who made it possible.

The new sound Rush brought to *Signals* confused friend and foe alike at the time of its release. *Rolling Stone* continued to insult even the idea of Rush with a typically nasty review. "Rush makes a strong argument for the view that advanced technology is not necessarily the same thing as progress," the reviewer stated. "Unfortunately," it continued, "they do so largely by screwing up." In its short review, *Rolling Stone* claimed the album to be "their most poppish yet" but, having traded their progressive and art credentials (which the magazine had always hated), the album is "mostly a wasted effort" with the music sounding like nothing more than "static."[50] No rational person would have expected anything kind from *Rolling Stone*, but even friends of Rush found the album perplexing. Mark Putterford of *Sounds* called it a "weak, below par album," filled with "DULL" songs.[51] *Kerrang!* explained the changes as a part of Rush accepting the "mantle of middle age" but warned that true Rush fans would "be sorely disappointed."[52]

---

1. Neil Peart, Foreword, to Joe Bergamini, *Taking Center Stage: A Lifetime of Live Performance*, Neil Peart (Milwaukee, WI: Hudson Music, 2012), 5.
2. Andy Tillison to author, personal correspondence, April 28, 2015.
3. Peart quoted in Robert Telleria, *Rush Tribute: Merely Players* (Kingston, ONT: Quarry Music Books, 2002), 156.
4. Rutkoski, "Interview: Neil Peart," *Rochester Freetime* (April 27–May 11, 1994).
5. "Interview with Neil Peart," *Rag* (May 1994).
6. Brad Wheeler, "A Rock-Solid Survivor in an Unpredictable World," *The Globe and Mail* (April 28, 2007), R5.
7. Neil Peart, "Personal Waves, The Story of an Album" [taken from: http://www.2112.net/powerwindows/main/RushInspirations.htm]
8. 110
    Popoff, *Contents Under Pressure*, 76; http://rushvault.com/2011/02/05/natural-science/; and http://www.2112.net/powerwindows/main/PeWlyrics.htm%5D
9. As a "going away" present (that is, heading to Austria for my sophomore year of college), my best friend, Kevin McCormick (to whom this book is dedicated), wrote out all of the lyrics of Natural Science for me. I carried that lyric sheet in my wallet for years, and the lyrics served as almost a prayer to me.
10. Keith Sharp, review of *Permanent Waves*, *Music Express* (February 1980).
11. *Permanent Waves* review, *Rolling Stone* (March 1, 1980).
12. Steve Pond, "Rush's Heavy-Metal Sludge," *Rolling Stone* (May 15, 1980).
13. "Intense Early Reaction to Rush's *Permanent Waves*," *RPM Weekly* (February 9, 1980).
14. Steve Gett, *Permanent Waves* review, *Melody Maker* (February 2, 1980).
15. Steve Rothery, quoted in Malcom Dome, "Rush: R40," *Prog* 52 (January 2015): 42
16. The original is Richard S. Foster, "A Nice Morning Drive," *Road and Track* (November 1973), 148–150.
17. Peart quoted in *Beyond the Lighted Stage*.
18. Lee quoted in *Beyond the Lighted Stage*.
19. Interview with Neil Peart, *Innerview with Jim Ladd*, June 11, 1981.
20. Peart, *Roadshow*, 84.
21. Peart, *Roadshow*, 85; and "Exclusive Interview with Neil Peart," *mikedolbear.com* (January 2006).
22. Peart in Dave Dickson, "Spirit of Peart," *Kerrang!* 44 (June 17–30/July 1–13, 1983).
23. Peart in Dave Dickson, "Spirit of Peart," *Kerrang!* 44 (June 17–30/July 1–13, 1983); and Lifeson in Rich Sutton, "On the Edge of the Limelight," *Song Hits* (November 1984). In the latter, Lifeson admits that all three members of Rush value their privacy, but "Neil the most." See also Greg Quill, "Neil Peart: New World Man," *Music Express* (September/October 1982).

24. "Interview: Neil Peart," *Modern Drummer* (April 1984).
25. Peart, *Roadshow*, 14.
26. Peart quoted in *Beyond the Lighted Stage*.
27. Peart, *Ghost Rider*, 34.
28. On Lee and family fleeing, see Nicholas Jennings, "Rock N Roll Royalty," *Maclean's* (September 30, 1991).
29. Lee, quoted in Steve Gett, "Touring Britain is a Grind," *Kerrang!* (October 21, 1982).
30. Basche, "Rush's Simpler 'Signals,'" *Circus* (November 30, 1982).
31. John Gill, "Take That, You Loon Panted Bigots," *Sounds* (February 14, 1981).
32. Andy Secher, "Rush to Glory," *Hit Parader* (April 1981).
33. Max Mobley, *Rush FAQ: All That's Left to Know About Rock's Greatest Power Trio* (Milwaukee, WI: Backbeat Records, 2014), 26.
34. Steve Gett, "New World Men," *Kerrang!* 26 (October 7, 1982).
35. Lee quoted in Menon, *Rush: An Oral History Uncensored*.
36. Raj Bahadur, "Rush Takes Off: The Geddy Lee Interview," *Northeast Ohio Scene* (October 28–November 3, 1982).
37. Lifeson quoted in Steve Gett, "New World Men," *Kerrang!* 26 (October 7, 1982).
38. Brian Harrigan, "Lifeson's Lifespan," *Melody Maker* (November 7, 1981); and Derek Oliver, "Rush Release," *Melody Maker* (May 5, 1984).
39. Steve Morse, "Sending New Signals, Rush on the Defense," *Boston Globe* (December 6, 1982).
40. Peart, *Traveling Music*, 46. In 1982, Peart had especially praised Ultravox's 1980 new wave masterpiece, *Vienna*. See Philip Basche, "Rush's Simpler Signals," *Circus* (November 30, 1982).
41. Mark Newman, "Canadian Rock and U.S. Rock Similar, Peart Says," *Grand Rapids Press*, November 7, 1982.
42. Basche, "Rush's Simpler 'Signals.'"
43. Pete Makowski, "Adrenalin Rush," *Sounds* (December 18, 1982).
44. Greg Quill, "Neil Peart: New World Man," *Music Express* (September/October 1982).
45. Interview with Neil Peart, "Signals Radio Premiere," September 1982.
46. Peart, *Roadshow*, 124–125.
47. Peart, "Stories from Signals: Collected from the Drummer's Diary," *Sounds* (October 16, 1982).
48. Peart, "Stories from Signals: Collected from the Drummer's Diary," *Sounds* (October 16, 1982).
49. Budofsky, *Modern Drummer Legends: Rush's Neil Peart*, 33.
50. J.D. Considine, *Signals* Album Review, *Rolling Stone* (October 28, 1982).
51. Mark Putterford, "Semi Flawed *Signals*," *Sounds* (September 11, 1982).
52. Dave Dickson, "A Rush of Old Age," *Kerrang!* (September 23–October 6, 1982).

A PERSONAL INTERLUDE
THE GRACE OF WINDOWS

1983–1986

My favorite Rush album has been, at least going back to April 1984, *Grace Under Pressure*. I realize that among Rush fans and among prog fans, this might be a surprising choice. My praise of *GUP* is not in any way meant to denigrate any other Rush albums. Frankly, I love them all. Rush has offered us an outrageous wealth of blessings, and I won't even pretend objectivity.

I love Rush. I love *Grace Under Pressure*.

I still remember opening *Grace Under Pressure* for the first time. Gently knifing the cellophane so as not to crease the cardboard, slowly pulling out the vinyl wrapped in a paper sleeve, the hues of gray, pink, blue, and granite and that egg caught in a vice grip, the distinctive smell of a brand-new album … the crackle as the needle hit …

I was sixteen.

From the opening wind-blown notes, sound effects, and sharp keyboard notes, I was hooked, completely. I had loved *Moving Pictures* and *Signals*—each giving me great comfort personally, perhaps even saving my life during some pretty horrific junior high and early high school moments.

But this *Grace Under Pressure*. This was something else.

If *Moving Pictures* and *Signals* taught me to be myself and pursue excellence, *Grace Under Pressure* taught me that once I knew myself, I had the high duty to go into the world and fight for what's good and right, no matter the cost. At sixteen, I desperately needed to believe that, and I thank God that Peart provided that lesson. There are so many other lessons a young energetic boy could have picked up from the rather fragile culture of the time and the incredibly dysfunctional home in which I was raised. With *Grace Under Pressure*, though, I was ready to follow Peart into Hell and back for the right cause. Peart certainly became one of the most foundational influences on my life, along with other authors I was reading at the time, such as Orwell and Bradbury.

Though I'm sure that Peart did not intend for the album to have any kind of overriding story such as the first sides of *2112* or *Hemispheres* had told, *Grace Under Pressure* holds together as a concept album brilliantly.

The opening calls to us: beware! Wake up! Shake off your slumbers! The world is near its doom.

Or so it seems.

Lee's voice, strong with anxiety, begins: "An ill wind comes arising …" In the pressures of chaos, Peart suggests, we so easily see the world fall apart, ourselves not only caught in the maelstrom, but possibly aggravating it. "Distant Early Warning" ends with possibly the most desperate cry of the Old Testament: "Absalom, Absalom!" Certainly, there is no hope merely in the self. Again, so it seems.

The second song, "Afterimage," gut-wrenching to the extreme, deals with the loss of a person, whose imprint is all that remains after the body is removed from this existence. Yet, despite the topic, there is more hope in this song than in the first. Despite loss, memory allows life to continue, to "feel the way you would." I had recently lost my maternal grandfather—the finest man I ever knew—before first hearing this album. His image will always be my "Afterimage."

It seems, though, that more than one have died. The third song, "Red Sector A," takes us into a prison camp. Whether a Holocaust camp or a Gulag, it's unclear. Frankly, it's probably not important if the owners of the camp are Communists or Fascists. Either way, those imprisoned inside are most likely doomed. Not only had I been reading lots of dystopian literature in 1984 (appropriate, I suppose, given the date), but I was reading everything I could find by and about the greatest of Soviet dissidents, Alexandr Solzhenitsyn. This made the Gulag even more real and more terrifying. Tyrannies of every shape cast a long shadow over the band, and the three members of Rush refused to let the memories of the twentieth century dismiss the horrors of concentration camps and killing fields. As Lee explained in an interview,

My parents were in Poland at the outset of the war, and the Germans came in, and every man they thought could be a threat to them they took out and shot. As the war moved on they were taken to a concentration camp. As the war got a little heavier, they were all moved to different concentration camps. My parents were sent to Auschwitz where they survived, which they thought was a miracle. When they got liberated—when the war was over—they didn't know what to do. They still lived in the concentration camp, as most people did, trying to collect themselves. When they liberated them, they thought they were the only people left in the world. Can you imagine that? They thought they were the few survivors. They were slowly informed that the world was still going on. Then they couldn't understand why they were saved. How could it happen? How could God let it happen? They gathered up what they could and came to Canada. They were going to go to New York, but someone said it was nice in Canada.[1]

Lifeson confirmed this, years later.

> *The first time I met Geddy's mum I saw her concentration camp number tattooed on her arm. That stayed with me. My parents came from Yugoslavia, and my father was in a work camp in Austria. The war affected everybody. Both my parents came to Canada as undocumented refugees. So Geddy and I shared a common background, and that really bonded us. Two Canadian-born Eastern Europeans whose parents had been displaced by the war.*[2]

Just when the brooding might become unbearable, the three men of Rush seem to offer a Gothic, not quite hellish, smile as the fourth song, "The Enemy Within" begins. Part One of "Fear," this fourth track of *Grace Under Pressure* offers a psychological insight into the paranoia of a person. Perhaps we should first look at our own problems before we place them whole cloth upon the world.

Pick needle up, turn album over, clean with dust sponge, and drop needle....

Funk. Sci-fi funk emerges after the needle has crackled and finds its groove. A robot has escaped, perhaps yearning for or even having attained sentience. I could never count how many hours of conversation these lyrics prompted, as Kevin McCormick and I discussed the nature of free will late into the night in our college dorm room.

It's the stuff of Philip K. Dick, the liberal arts, and the best of theology.

More bass funk for track six and a return to psychological introspection, "Kid Gloves." But we move out quickly into the larger world again with the seventh track, "Red Lenses," taking the listener back to the themes of paranoia. When the man emerges for action, as in the final track of Grace Under Pressure, "Beneath the Wheels," will he do so in reaction to the personal pain he has experienced, or will he do so with an objective truth set to enliven the common good?

In the end, this is the choice for those who do not lose themselves to the cathode rays. Is man fighting for what should be, or is he reacting merely to what has happened, "to live between a rock and a hard place"?

Unlike the previous albums which end with narrative certainty, *Grace Under Pressure* leaves the listener with more questions than it answers, though tellingly it harkens to Hemingway and to T.S. Eliot. Given the album as a whole, one might take this as Stoic resignation—merely accepting the flaws of the world. "Can you spare another war—another waste land?"

Wheels can take you around
Wheels can cut you down.
Got to try and fill the void.

But, this doesn't fit Peart. We all know whatever blows life has dealt Peart, he has stood back up, practiced twenty times harder, and read thirty more books. That man does not go down for long.

And, neither should we.

In the spring of 1987, much to my surprise, one of my humanities professors allowed me to write on the ideas of Peart. I can no longer find that essay (swallowed up and now painfully lonely on some primitive Mac Plus hard drive or 3.5" floppy disk, most likely rotting in a landfill in central Kansas), but it was the kind of writing and thinking that opened up whole new worlds to me. My only quotes were from *Grace Under Pressure*, drawing a distinction between the nature of the liberal arts and the loss of humanity through the mechanizing of the human person. It dealt, understandably, with environmental and cultural degradation, the dangers of conformist thinking, and the brutal inhumanity of ideologies. It was probably the smartest thing I'd written up to that point in my life, and even my professor liked it enough to award me an A.

Of course, the ideas were all Peart's, and I fondly imagined him as that really great older brother—the one who knows what an annoying pain I am, but who sees promise in me anyway, giving me just enough space to find my own way.

Geoff Barton returned from a hiatus to review the album, calling *Grace Under Pressure* "the latest link in a truly lustrous chain."[3] *Sounds* gave it four out of five stars, noting that Rush "are making graceful sweeping advances and this album shows just how versatile they are and how much they have got to offer. I have the strangest feeling that I've only scraped away at the surface of this record."[4] And, of course, *Rolling Stone* rained on the parade.

The problem, though, is musical. On the record, the lack of melody and any but the most rudimentary harmonic development soon becomes oppressive. In addition, Alex Lifeson is not a particularly interesting lead guitarist, and the strictures of the trio format still result in more splattery drum bashing than you'll ever care to hear. Rush delivers the goods, all right: strong social statements enveloped in a massive, pounding sound. But it's old news, and old music, too.[5]

POWER WINDOWS

Everywhere I turned that fall of 1985—in ways far more than any other Rush song since "Tom Sawyer"—I heard "The Big Money." MTV played the video repeatedly (we didn't have MTV, but friends did), and our wonderful local radio station—KICT95 out of Wichita—had it in constant rotation. Of course, being a massively obsessed Rush fan since first encountering them in seventh grade detention, I was thrilled to see Rush get so much attention. Sadly, though, I became overly saturated with "The Big Money." It's the only Rush song that has ever grown tiring for me. For years, it sat down there with "Stairway to Heaven." I just shut both out of my mind, flipped the radio dial when either played. As *Power Windows* is one of my all-time favorite albums, this has been rather difficult for me to accomplish. For nearly two decades, though, I started the album with the second track, "Grand Designs."

Then on September 18, 2012, at the Palace in Auburn Hills, Michigan, standing next to my good friend and student, Dom, Rush played it as the second track of the *Clockwork Angels* tour. Straight from "Subdivisions" to "The Big Money" to "Force Ten" and then, three songs from *Power Windows* in a row: "Grand Designs"; "Middle-town Dreams"; and "Territories." Half of the album! It was brilliant. Poor Dom. He was only a college student, and he had to hear my sound-bite reminiscences for every track. I was reliving a huge part of my high school experience during that concert.

Seeing "The Big Money" live made me realize why that song is so wonderful. Lifeson, Lee, and Peart brought immense energy to it (and "Force Ten," as well—the most rocking version I'd heard from Rush; Alex even played one of his best guitar solos for this song on this tour). Suddenly, whatever tiredness and reluctance I'd felt about "The Big Money" over the last several decades dissipated at the moment the opening few notes began in Auburn Hills. Add video of spinning and printing dollars as well as the Three Stooges, and I was sold. Really, everything was perfect—the drumming, the bass, the guitar solo. And, of course, the *Austin Powers* moment at the end of the performance: "One million dollars!"

Now as I write this, I'm back in those autumnal days of 1985. Let "The Big Money" reign.

But the point of this interlude is not to praise "The Big Money" specifically, but to remember *Power Windows*. I'm happy to praise both! And frankly, I've been offering praise of *Power Windows* since it came out, despite my caveat for "The Big Money." Now, I realize how wrong I was. The whole thing deserves praise, and one cannot separate any song from the whole. It is what it is, and it's a thing of immense beauty.

In *Contents Under Pressure* by Martin Popoff, Peart argues that he sees *Power Windows* and *Hold Your Fire* as two sides of the same coin, separate from *Grace Under Pressure*, but also from *Presto*. Certainly, there's an argument to be made here. In terms of bass and drums, *Power Windows* and *Hold Your Fire* have the most distinctly jazz feel of any Rush albums. At times, taking the rhythm section alone, the listener might be enjoying a Chick Corea album from the same time period. In production, though, *Power Windows* comes across as rather raw power, while *Hold Your Fire* feels rather lush. Whatever similarities—and there are many—the albums seem very different to the listener. As Neil states, the first is an extrovert, the second an introvert.

As a fan, though, I tend to hear consistent themes in *Moving Pictures* through *Hold Your Fire*. From my perspective, *Moving Pictures* stresses the need to be an individual against the crowd; *Signals* warns that being such an individual will cause pain, but is worth it; *Grace Under Pressure* deals with recovery from such persecution (sometimes in the hallway, sometimes in the concentration camp); *Power Windows* deals with excellence against conformity; and *Hold Your Fire* pleads for restraint in the now comfortable individual looking at those he's made uncomfortable.

Granted, these themes are autobiographical for me, in the sense that I grew up with them, and each album played a key role in my own understanding of the world. That is, these themes might not have been intended by Peart, and I may be alone in seeing them this way. As I've mentioned before, Neil Peart has influenced me as much as anyone in my life—ranging from Plato (I teach western civ for a living, so allow me a little pretense here) to St. Paul to my mother. Plato-Paul-Peart!!! The three Ps.

In terms of wordplay, Neil is at his best on *Power Windows*.

In "The Big Money," Peart considers the good and the evils of what we now refer to quite commonly as "Crony Capitalism." As with much of this album, the shadow of cultural critic, socialist-turned-libertarian and anti-war novelist John Dos Passos, hangs over "The Big Money." Dos Passos also called his style "The Camera Eye." 1936's *The Big Money* concluded Dos Passos's famous USA Trilogy. Much like Peart, Dos Passos traveled incessantly, offering a fine cultural criticism over everything he surveyed.

"Grand Designs," track two, comes from the final part of the "District of Columbia" trilogy published by Dos Passos in 1949. It examines individual genius in line with nature and individual genius against nature. In the conflict of style and substance, Peart is also referencing the grand Anglo-American poet, T.S. Eliot, and his 1925 poem *The Hollow Men*.

The third track, "Manhattan Project," anticipates the history-telling prog of Big Big Train, offering a rather neutral analysis of the development of the first three atomic bombs. Interestingly enough for Peart, he continues to harken back to religious language and themes, especially Catholic, referring again and again to "a world without end." Peart spent a considerable amount of time researching the background information for the song and found the process fascinating. "Then I had to distill all of that knowledge into what would add up to only 167 words—and they had to be words that could be sung."[6]

"Marathon" echoes a number of other Peart songs, but it does it with extraordinary energy. A celebration of the battle of the Athenians over the Persians in the fifth century, BC, it also deals with the virtue of fortitude. "I'm a big Rush fan, and my favorite track is probably 'Marathon' from *Power Windows* which, for me, was their last truly great album," Galahad composer and front man, Stu Nicholson has stated. "We actually used to play that song in local pubs in the early days of Galahad, which raised an eyebrow or two as it was such a big sound, especially for the time."[7]

"Territories" offers a scathing criticism of propaganda, nationalisms, and nation states. In his criticisms and clever examples, Peart echoes the anti-statism of Mark Twain. In his writing, Peart has always shied away from anything even hinting at nationalism or jingoism. In 1982, he told an interviewer that if the US and Canada abolished their mutual border, he would gladly move to the US—a move he eventually made decades later.[8]

Most likely taking the title of the following track from the famous 1925 sociological report of Muncie, Indiana, entitled *Middletown*, Peart explores the dark secrets of small towns. Not surprisingly, given the state of sociology in the 1920s, the report considers the everyday habits and desires of rural Americans. In his own "Middletown," Peart examines the life of rural America as well as the generally unfulfilled dreams of those wishing to escape.

"Emotion Detector" is one of Peart's most Stoic songs, offering something against both the extremes of optimism and the cynicism of despair. In the end, in a common Peart theme, man must restrain his reaction toward others, recognizing that one does not need external validation, should integrity already exist in the original act. A true man judges himself.

The final and most proggish/artistic song of the album is "Mystic Rhythms." Rush ends with wonder at the intense diversity of the world and of all of the universe.

By now in Rush's career, not only were a lot of music journalists taking notice of the band—a few years behind the fans—but they were also taking Rush more seriously than ever before. *Billboard* offered its utterly positive take.

The Canadian trio's polished yet vivid rock continues to balance its musical muscle against thoughtful lyric concerns, and this latest set finds percussionist/lyricist Neil Peart discoursing on nationalism, greed, mysticism and the Bomb. If such themes are lofty by current AOR and mainstream pop standards, the energetic playing, which again juggles the band's early progressive rock instincts with newer electronic elements, and Geddy Lee's soaring vocal signature should keep the faith with their platinum constituency.[9]

For the first time in its history, *Rolling Stone* gave a positive review of the album, though failing to offer a rating. What especially impressed the magazine was the ability of Rush to mix "Yes and the Sex Pistols."[10]

Finding a producer for *Power Windows* proved difficult at first. After replacing the long-lived Terry Brown (every album up through *Signals*) with Peter Henderson (*Grace Under Pressure*), Rush found their third producer in Peter Collins, best known for his work with Nik Kershaw and Blancmange. Making the connection to Britain even stronger, Rush recorded much of the album at Abbey Road Studios and in parts of London. They also worked with Anne Dudley of the Art of Noise, who directed the strings. For whatever reason, every member of Rush and their road crew and team earn a nickname. Terry Brown as "Broon"; Neil Peart as "Pratt"; Geddy Lee as "Dirk"; Alex Lifeson as "Lerxst." Welcomed fully into the Rush family, Collins became "Mr. Big," for his enormous 1980s sound production.[11]

Though *Power Windows* rocks with full force throughout most of the album (the final track, "Mystic Rhythms," being the very proggy standout), it has also a strange new wave feel to it. Ok, this needs explaining. Neil and Geddy sound as though they're playing in a rocking jazz band from the 1980s, but Alex sounds as though he could be playing for The Fixx. Alex, like Jamie West-Oram, seems to be creating immense but punctuated guitarscapes. One of the things that makes *Power Windows* so effective, is this strange but powerful synthesis of jazz bass and drums with new wave guitar. In ways that *Drama* attempted to be for Yes in 1980 (some of the same production crew worked on both), *Power Windows* succeeds at bridging prog, rock, new wave, and jazz. I think *Drama* is a fine album (in fact, a favorite), but I think that *Power Windows* is truly successful at this attempt to bridge genres. Perhaps *Power Windows* couldn't have come about without *Drama* first, but an exploration of this would be well beyond the intent of this book.

Suffice it to say, I love both.

1. Scott Cohen, "Geddy Lee: From Immigrants' Song to Rush's Lead Singer," *Circus* (October 27, 1977).
2. James McNair, "New World Man" [Interview with Alex Lifeson], Planet Rock (April 2019), 90.
3. Geoff Barton, "Pressure Points," *Kerrang!* (April 5–18, 1984).
4. Jay Williams, "Grace and Favour," *Sounds* (April 21, 1984).
5. Kurt Loder, *Grace Under Pressure* review, *Rolling Stone* (June 21, 1984).
6. Peart, *Far and Away*, 182.
7. Stu Nicholson, quoted in Malcom Dome, "Rush: R40," *Prog* 52 (January 2015): 44
8. Mark Newman, "Canadian Rock and U.S. Rock Similar, Peart Says," *Grand Rapids Press* (November 7, 1982).
9. Christa Titus, "Spotlight Review: *Power Windows*," *Billboard* (November 2, 1985).
10. David Fricke, *Power Windows* review, *Rolling Stone* (January 30, 1986).
11. Mr. Big was also the name of a band that toured with Rush during the 1980s.

3 TIME AND MOTION
1987–1996

On September 8, 1987, Rush released *Hold Your Fire*, an album of short prog gems, each brimming with jazz-fusion rhythms and dense production. Layer upon layer. Once again asking Peter Collins to produce, this would prove to be the band's last album with their longtime label, Mercury. Though the album holds a few '80s flourishes, such as Aimee Mann's guest vocals, *Hold Your Fire* has qualities that make it timeless in ways that better known Rush albums, such as *Moving Pictures*, are not. Even the critics liked this one, though only a few actually reviewed the album. Steffan Chirazi of *Kerrang!* and Paul Elliot of *Sounds* each gave it a perfect rating, arguing "This is another major Rush strength that *Hold Your Fire* illustrates, Rush's ability to advance and experiment without becoming pompous or indulgent."[1] Chirazi ended the review by demanding that all lovers of music purchase the album immediately. "Rush are more relevant now than they've ever been. And they keep getting better," Elliot concluded.[2]

The title, *Hold Your Fire*, presents an album that, at least topically, is as Aristotelian as Peart ever gets. In its expression of activity (fire), it is actually a call for prudence, restraint, and even resignation. This call comes across in every one of the ten tracks of the fifty-minute album.

"Force 10," not surprisingly given its name, offers an opening storm of fusion. Beginning with a choir on a sustained, quavering note and with odd percussion sounds that resembled weaponized Ping-Pong balls, *Hold Your Fire* blisters on the first track. With lyrics co-written with longtime friend and ally, Pye Dubois, "Force 10" provides a look at the whirligig of the world:

We can rise and fall like empires
Flow in and out like the tide
Be vain and smart, humble and dumb
We can hit and miss like pride
We can circle around like hurricanes
Dance and dream like lovers
Attack the day like birds of prey
Or scavengers under cover
We can move with savage grace
To the rhythms of the night
Cool and remote like dancing girls
In the heat of the beat and the lights
We can wear the rose of romance
An air of joie de vivre
Too-tender hearts upon our sleeves
Or skin as thick as thieves'

However we approach such a mess, we must always remain honest. If anything, the harder the world, the harder the truth, the greater our duty to speak it.

A song embracing middle age (though the members of the band were only in their middle thirties), "Time Stand Still" captures the nostalgia of the "The Analog Kid" but with wisdom rather than longing. Much to the surprise and chagrin of long-time Rush fans, the band even invited pop singer, Aimee Mann, to contribute backing vocals. Her sweet voice only adds to the emotional power of the song. The lyrics ask one to capture the moment—past and present—rather than dwelling only in the past.

Freeze this moment a little bit longer
Make each sensation a little bit stronger
Experience slips away ...
Make each impression a little bit stronger
Freeze this motion a little bit longer
The innocence slips away ...
Summer's going fast
Nights growing colder
Children growing up—
Old friends growing older
Experience slips away ...

In an interview with the *Boston Globe*, Peart stated:

All through the '70s our lives were flying by; we spent so much time on the road that it became like a dark tunnel. You start to think about the people you're neglecting, friends and family. So the song is about stopping to enjoy that; with a warning against too much looking back. Instead of getting nostalgic about the past, it's more a plea for the present.[3]

Track three, "Open Secrets," has a painful feel to it. More direct than usual about male-female relations, Peart describes the agony of marital misunderstanding. "It went right by me," the song laments.

I was looking out the window
I should have looked at your face instead

Peart understands that there is communication at a deeper level than mere words—that rationality may say one thing, while instincts, defensiveness, and pride all state another.

Taken directly from Aristotle's understanding of virtue, "Second Nature" refers to the habituation of goodness. That is, the profound Greek philosopher asks us to make our goodness so routine that it becomes a part of us. "Prime Nature" could be a gift directly from creation itself. "Second Nature," however, relies on the will of man, recognizing man's ability to habituate the good.

A memo to a higher office
Open letter to the powers-that-be
To a god, a king, a head of state
A captain of industry
To the movers and the shakers—
Can't everybody see?
It ought to be second nature—
I mean, the places where we live!
Let's talk about this sensibly—
We're not insensitive
I know that progress has no patience—
But something's got to give

This song serves as a sequel to "Closer to the Heart." While that song relied on American classical liberal philosophy as expressed by Thomas Jefferson and Benjamin Franklin, this one has as much Henry David Thoreau as it does Greek philosophy.[4]

Continuing the direct reference to Greek philosophy on track five, "Prime Mover," Aristotle's name for god, Peart explores all motion and activity in the world. Unlike his teacher Plato, who imagined god as the perfect being, a Celestial King who contemplated the true, the good, and the beautiful, Aristotle's god set the world in motion by an action of love. His very thought sent love (purpose) into the universe. "Nature, according to our theory," Aristotle argued, "makes nothing in vain." In other words, not a single thing in the created order—no person, no tree, no cheetah—exists without purpose.[5] One never knows the purpose of a thing with free will, however, until that thing is tested in community.

Alternating currents in a tidewater surge
Rational resistance to an unwise urge
Anything can happen
From the point of conception
To the moment of Truth
At the point of surrender
To the burden of proof
From the point of ignition to the final drive
The point of the journey is not to arrive
Anything can happen

Track six, "Lock and Key," explores the hidden desires we all have. Again following the ideas of Aristotle, Peart recognizes that a thing such as anger is natural. Used properly, our anger becomes righteous and corrects injustice. Used poorly, it can lead to rage and even murder. Mixing philosophy with psychology, Peart asks how we suppress the worst within each of us. "Behind the finer things—the civilized veneer—the heart of a lonely hunter/guards a dangerous frontier."

What could be part II of "Marathon" on *Power Windows*, track seven of *Hold Your Fire*, "Mission," calls for us to persevere in our best, in our excellence, in our search for a proper order.

When I feel the powerful visions
Their fire has made alive
I wish I had that instinct
I wish I had that drive

"Mission" remains one of Rush's most inspirational tracks,

and the live performance of it—with a slightly faster beat and a deeper resonance—is even more moving than the original studio version.

Track eight, "Turn the Page," another driving rocker, laments the confusion of the world. How do we respond to disaster after disaster? How do we sympathize with those we don't know, whatever horrors have entered their lives? Overwhelmed, we simply turn the page of the newspaper, moving on to yet another mishap. And, yet, no matter how detached we might be from such tragedies, we are each connected to one another, for "nothing survives in a vacuum." Truth, Peart writes of our postmodern understanding is "after all a moving target."

The final two tracks of the album, almost infinitely mellow and Aquarian, serve as a coda to *Hold Your Fire*. Track nine, "Tai-Shan," considers the mystical heritage of China. A cross between "Countdown" and "Mystic Rhythms"—but in Zen-like peace—the song describes Peart's experiences at a holy mountain. The final song, "High Water," follows the rhythm of the tide, progressing from lulling to intense frenzy. Lifeson's guitar especially captures and precipitates the mood as the song builds. The lyrics depict not only the natural movements of tide, but the tides within our familial and personal histories and memories. "We still feel that relation/when the water takes us home."

Giving the album a five out of five, the reviewer for *Sounds* wrote:

> There's nothing cold or clichéd here. Unlike Deep Purple and their half-croaked contemporaries, Rush have long since dropped the grubby melodrama and woken up to the late '80s. Settled and polished they may be, but Rush are more relevant now than they've ever been. And they keep getting better.[6]

As noted above, *Kerrang!* also gave it a perfect rating.[7]

PRESTO

Less than two weeks after thousands of Germans tore down the Berlin Wall, Rush released its album, *Presto*, thus inaugurating Rush 2.2. Going for a sleeker, less dense sound, Rush 2.2 witnessed the band embrace more straightforward rock, but they were also significantly influenced by pop, hip-hop, and Seattle grunge. *Presto* appeared on November 21, 1989; *Roll the Bones* on September 3, 1991; and *Counterparts* on October 19, 1993. The albums get progressively harder and edgier, in sound and in lyrics. Interestingly enough, the band even hired Rupert Hine, best known for his work with new wave acts The Fixx and Howard Jones, to produce *Presto* and *Roll the Bones*. Never before or after *Presto* has the band sounded so pop-friendly. Even the album cover designed by Syme is warm and fuzzy, a number of very friendly, huggable rabbits emerging from a top hat in an almost Easter-like setting. Magic meets Christianity meets paganism.

Presto was also Rush's first album after leaving their first record label, Mercury. From the band's perspective, Mercury had simply taken the band for granted, never putting too much into them nor even expecting too much from them.[8] After fifteen years with Mercury, they joined Atlantic Records, recording six full-length studio albums with them, along with the tribute CD, *Feedback* (2004). Asked in 1989 how this change in label might change the dynamic of Rush, Peart answered frankly.

No, to the contrary, I think it's up to them to prove it. We've had a lot of albums that have done pretty well. Atlantic, our new label, is convinced that they can do better for us. We're not saying, "Sign us because we'll sell more records with you." They're saying, "Sign with us because we'll sell more records." It's a pretty simple thing. It doesn't put any pressure on us at all, any more than we already place on ourselves, which is serious enough.[9]

Lyrically, Peart explores the role of appearances on *Presto*. In the first track, "Show Don't Tell," he takes the role of judge and jury, considering the actions of a person, perhaps himself, in which he analyzes the intent of a statement and the consequent actions. In the second track, "Chain Lightning," the lyrics offer the question of how a rock creates ripples in a pool, but with the imagery of light and astronomical phenomena.

Sun dogs fire on the horizon
Meteor rain stars across the night
This moment may be brief
But it can be so bright
Reflected in another source of light

Peart tries to capture the moment, crystalizing it in eternity. The third track, "The Pass," deals rather movingly with the subject of teen suicide.

Keeping with the topic of youth, "War Paint" examines the way we decorate ourselves before encountering our peers and the communities in which we find ourselves. With the best and the most driving of the tracks of the album, "Scars," Peart wonders how emotional tragedies and victories build upon one another, building a sort of shield upon our soul and emotions. Some become calloused and some disappear.

The following track offers a grand wish, "If I could wave my magic wand." There's no reason to doubt that Peart would love to make all well in the world, and in the song, he offers a sort of love note to the universe, a thankfulness for merely being alive. The strangest song, musically, is "Super Conductor," a reflection on fame, its delusions, and its horrors. "Anagram (for Mongo)," track 8, is playful, taking its title from the Mel Brooks film, *Blazing Saddles*.

The final three songs offer one of the most riveting and cohesive conclusions to any Rush album: "Red Tide," "Hand Over Fist," and "Available Light." It's these final three songs that have most successfully blended the raw energy and enthusiasm of Rush with the controlled and sleek production of Rupert Hine, one track bleeding into another. Lee's voice has never sounded more mature and confident. Hine clearly knew how to get the most out of it.

"Red Tide" presents a prophetic warning about the state of the world, a sequel to *Grace Under Pressure*, while romantically calling for us to "not go gently into the endless winter night," paraphrasing the Celtic poet Dylan Thomas's famous poem from 1951. "Hand over Fist" brings the listener back to childhood, but with a recognition that childish games should remain in the hands of children. As an adult, we must be more willing to embrace the strange and the stranger. The final song, "Available Light," one of the most powerful in Rush's career, begins with a sort of nightclub jazz piano, and builds into a theatric anthem, a call to enjoy the beauties of the world without believing that the tricks of light are themselves reality.

Run to light from shadow
Sun gives me no rest
Promise offered in the east
Broken in the west
Chase the sun around the world
I want to look at life
In the available light.

These are possibly Peart's most poetic lyrics, given form by Lee's vocal convictions. In these lyrics, the writer has lived up to what T.E. Hulme, T.S. Eliot, and the founders of the poetic medium Imagism wanted to achieve almost a century earlier.[10] As with Imagism, each word connects to every other word, an allegory for the human person in life, each connected to every other, past, present, and future.

ROLL THE BONES

Two years later, employing the same producer, Hine, Rush released one of its most eclectic albums, *Roll the Bones*. Less sleek than its predecessor, at least musically, and with lyrics far more philosophical than poetic, the album begins with "Dreamline," a solid rock outing. Almost a mission statement for the album, itself dealing with luck, free will, and providence, it contains one of Peart's finest and most thought-provoking lines: "We're only immortal for a limited time." Rush offers a sublimely powerful version of the song in concert.

The second track, the rock-pop song "Bravado," contains few surprises musically. In terms of meaning, though, Peart retells the story of Icarus, claiming it is worth it to burn our wings in the attempt to better ourselves and defy the gods as well as the fates. Even in loss, there is victory, if we give everything we have. "We will pay the price/But we will not count the cost."

Most shockingly to the music world, Rush incorporated a very Canadian rap in the third track, the namesake of the album. In a purely Aristotelian manner, the words declare: "Why are we here?/Because we're here." Reality exists. Accept this and deal with it. In many ways, this is a kinder version of "Anthem" and "Something for Nothing."

Following a similar message, track four demands that the listener "Face Up," literally accepting whatever wild card appears in the hand, symbolically accepting reality. "Where's My Thing?" (track five) is the first instrumental for Rush since "YYZ" ten years earlier, and also their first song since "YYZ" to earn a Grammy nomination.

The following track, "The Big Wheel," comes back to the themes of fate and free will. A reference to the wheel of chance one might find at a carnival, the "Big Wheel" also seems to refer to Huck Finn's travels down the Mississippi, encountering each new situation with frankness and humor. A third meaning comes from the cycles of the seasons: winter, spring, summer, and fall.

In one of his most political anti-political moments, "Heresy," Peart decries the history of communism, throwing up his hands in frustration, "What was it all about?" The world of ideology is "dull" and "grey." As he explained in a 1997 interview,

As far as the future is concerned, I wouldn't dare to predict it. The greatest changes in modern times would never have been foreseen twenty years ago, by anyone—the dismantling of the Berlin Wall, the collapse of the Soviet Union, the rise of the minivan, and certainly the spread of this particular "bone of contention," the Internet.[11]

The title of this song reveals much about Peart's own individualism, which has become somewhat religious (of an informal sort) and spiritual for him. Interestingly enough, his drum pattern used in the song comes from a rhythm he first heard when traveling in the African country of Togo.[12]

If anything, Peart's hatred of ideologies had grown, a quarter of a century after the destruction of the Berlin Wall. "It's a safe bet," he writes, "that no individual in history has been the cause of so much suffering as Karl Marx."[13] One of his fondest hopes is that what happened to communism will happen to organized religion. "It seemed—and seems—outrageous that the entire planet endured decades of anxiety, not to mention all the stunted lives in these Shadowlands, under the totalitarian boot-heel, for the sake of some misguided ideology," he writes. Then, adding parenthetically, "Someday, I trust, the same will be said about religion."[14] As Peart understood it, religion is simply another "ism" which delimits our free will, brainwashing us from our earliest days, into a sort of restricted and aborted humanity.[15]

The track that follows, "The Ghost of a Chance," is a rationalist love song.[16] We meet our loved one by accident, but we make or break our relationship by choice. How many choices had to be made at any point in history for two people to come together? Throughout the song, Peart de-mystifies love. If the rap in the first half of the album is Canadian, pure and simple, the rap/spoken word in the second to last song of *Roll the Bones*, "Neurotica," is psychological.

Snap!
Snap!
Hide in your shell, let the world go to hell
It's like Russian roulette to you
Snap!
Sweat running cold, you can't face growing old
It's a personal threat to you
Snap!
The world is a cage for your impotent rage
But don't let it get to you
Snap!

The final track, "You Bet Your Life," returns to the central theme of the album. Reality is real. Take your chances, and do the best you can. It also, however, contains a kind of rap/spoken word moment. This time, however, the rap is purely academic.

Anarchist reactionary running dog revisionist
Hindu Muslim catholic creation/evolutionist
Rational romantic mystic cynical idealist
Minimal expressionist post-modern neo-symbolist
Armchair rocket scientist graffiti existentialist
Deconstruction primitive performance photo-realist
Be-bop or a one-drop or a hip-hop lite-pop-metallist
Gold adult contemporary urban country capitalist

This rap is so mocking of labels that Peart seems almost to be crying foul against every person and critic who has ever tried to trap the band with a dismissive and confining description or label.

COUNTERPARTS

In 1993, Rush released *Counterparts*, hailed by friend and foe alike as a return to form. If nothing else, the guitars are heavy, and Lee avoids rapping. Lee viewed it as "a big turning point in reconnecting with the kind of rock and roll guts of Rush."[17] Of the albums in Rush 2.3, *Counterparts* is the grungiest, the most influenced by then-thriving bands such as Pearl Jam, Soundgarden, Stone Temple Pilots, and Live. Based in large part on the philosophical and metaphysical writings of the Swiss psychologist Carl Jung as well as on the literature of T.S. Eliot, the album considers the various sides of a group as well as of a person. Being Jungian, it is also Platonic, considering substance and shadow, existence and shade.

Peart spent months researching the lyrics for the album, diving into what was then the very beginning of gender studies. In his research, he encountered a person who held a position in academia comparable to his own in the music world, Camille Paglia. After reading even the smallest bit of Paglia—such as her *Sexual Personae* (1990) or *Sex, Art, and American Culture* (1992)—it becomes readily apparent how strongly she shaped Peart's lyrics for *Counterparts*.

Trained in the classics and greats of the western tradition, Paglia embraced libertarianism to the fullest extent possible in issues dealing with sexuality. She calls for a complete decriminalization of all sexual acts with the exception of rape. Liberalism foolishly "expects government to provide materially for all, a feat manageable only by an expansion of authority and a swollen bureaucracy." Consequently, she continues, liberals see government as a "tyrant father," but hope it will act as a "nurturing mother."[18]

Even more importantly, a woman, she argues, is naturally very different from a man and must be recognized as such.

I have found the words masculine and feminine indispensable for my notations of appearance and behavior, but I apply them freely to both sexes, according to mood and situation. Here are my conclusions, after a lifetime of observation and reflection. Maleness at its hormonal extreme is an angry, ruthless density of self, motivated by a principle of "attack." Femaleness at its hormonal extreme is first an acute sensitivity of response, literally thin-skinned (a hormonal effect in women), and secondly a stability, composure, and self-containment, a slowness approaching the sultry. Biologically, the male is impelled toward restless movement; his moral danger is brutishness. Biologically, the female is impelled toward waiting, expectancy; her moral danger is stasis. Androgen agitates; estrogen tranquilizes—hence the drowsiness and "glow" of pregnancy. Most of us inhabit not polar extremes but a constantly shifting great middle. However, a preponderance of gray does not disprove the existence of black and white. Sexual geography, our body image, alters our perception of the world. Man is contoured for invasion, while woman remains the hidden, a cave of archaic darkness. No legislation or grievance committee can change these eternal facts.[19]

Reading these words makes the whole of *Counterparts* fall together, lyrically and artistically. Songs that seem disparate in meaning—such as "Animate" and "Nobody's Hero"—become whole when seen through the lens of Peart reading Paglia. Indeed, it becomes rather clear that Peart (and Syme through the artwork) had fully embraced the work of Paglia, placing her literary and philosophical theories in a pure rock format. Paglia, it should be noted, loves rock music, seeing it as the most important movement in the history of Romanticism, a full-blown blast and rebirth of paganism in a syncretic, post-Christian world.[20]

Many critics have decried Paglia as an anti-feminist feminist. Certainly, her own take on feminism is, at best, eccentric. A feminism that calls for equality between the sexes is merely wishful thinking, she claims, and ultimately is just another form of Western Puritanism. It's also downright dangerous for society and especially for males. Like all systems of equality, a feminism of this sort only makes all of us weaker. A devoted Nietzschean, Paglia wants a society of excellence and competition. Her heroes are Elizabeth Taylor—endowed by nature with a goddess's body and charisma—and Madonna. Each has taken the pagan and exploded it to a form of divine madness. In her mind, art should be edgy, creative, unrestricted by the market or the norms. Art should be a form of constant melodrama, a liturgy that demands full immersion by artist, witness, and critic. "The greatest honor that can be paid to the artwork, on its pedestal of ritual display, is to describe it with sensory completeness," she writes, thus advocating the tangibility of art itself, a thing to be absorbed not merely gazed upon.[21]

In *Sexual Personae*, a work of painstaking scholarship and a myriad of opinions, Paglia argues that "society is an artificial construction, a defense against nature's power."[22] Nature thinks poorly of humanity, it seems, and humans developed the rituals of religion as a way to placate and attenuate the wrath of the elements. In particular, Christianity is little more than a re-packaged "sky cult."[23] In homage to such a view, Paglia lists de Sade, Nietzsche, and Freud as the greatest thinkers of the modern era. These three, she believes, are the true men of the West.[24]

Like Peart, Paglia journeyed wherever the ideas, the research, and the logic led, regardless of what the in-crowd thought.

"Her odyssey has been much like mine," Peart says. "She came out of '60s feminism, so her credentials are sound. Then her study, basically 25 years of scholarship, led her to certain conclusions that people dismiss with a snap. She spends years and years studying something and then says, 'There's this and this difference between males and females,' and somebody says, 'No there isn't.' This bothers me, too. If somebody's not willing to do the homework on it, then they have no right to the opinion."[25]

As Peart clarified, just as Paglia did not claim a full acceptance of Freud's ideas, he did not fully accept Paglia's either. Yet, she had brains and gumption, and Peart appreciated her for these things.²⁶

The artwork, conceptualized and designed by Peart and Syme, is some of the densest and most involved of Rush albums. Though the cover depicts a simplistic and almost sophomoric sexual image—a bolt entering a nut—the interior of the album is packed with dualistic and triple-istic images: see no evil, hear no evil, speak no evil; a rabbit and hare; paper, scissors, rock; yin and yang; male and female; etc. Even the very layout—from simple on the outside to complex on the inside—explains much about the album as well as about Peart and Rush.

The opening song, the punchy "Animate," allows Peart to explore the many nuances and complications of the human psyche. Without knowing the Jungian background, one might reasonably assume that Rush had embraced a sort of New Age/tarot philosophy.

Goddess in my garden
Sister in my soul
Angel in my armor
Actress in my role
Daughter of a demon lover
Empress of the hidden face
Priestess of the pagan mother
Ancient queen of inner space

Though one can find the images employed in the works of Jung, one can more readily find them used in Paglia's *Sexual Personae*. In all of her writings, she utilizes New Age and astrological signs as a way of making the pagan normal and reversing and undoing much of the Christian baptism of pagan things, places, and moments.

As though responding violently to the more delicate confessional tone of "Animate," "Stick It Out" (track two) is purely phallic and brimming over with testosterone. As with some of the songs on the previous two albums, Peart wants the listener to admit his faults, accept them as a part of his being, and deal with them openly. Self-deception only leads to greater insecurities and greater personal immoralities. Only full disclosure and acceptance of a fault leads to its attenuation and even reversal. The third track, "Cut to the Chase," examines the "motor of the western world," raw creativity and genius. With appropriate limitations and delimitations, it can remake the world for good. Unharnessed and untamed, it can turn the world upside down.

Track four, "Nobody's Hero," deals very frankly with human sexuality and, somewhat jarringly and clumsily, homosexuality. Possibly the greatest of all progressive metal artists, the Dutchman Arjen Lucassen, believes this to be Rush's finest moment.

Their late '80s "synthesizer period" was not my cup of tea, but for me, Counterparts *was an excellent return to form. In fact, the song "Nobody's Hero" from* Counterparts *is probably my most treasured Rush song overall. I love the chord structure and the catchy melodies, coupled with Geddy's great soothing vocals and Neil Peart's thought-provoking lyrics about homosexuality and AIDS.*[27]

The song also deals with other themes as well—in particular the difference between a true and honest heroism and the illusion of heroism.

"Between the Sun and Moon," the fifth track, considers all of the spaces in between the things of substance. The sun is a point of focus, as is the moon, but one must also recognize the vast space between the two, understanding the connection as a mystery.

Just as bluntly as "Nobody's Hero" dealt with sexuality, "Alien Shore," the sixth track, looks at the tenuous hold a husband and wife have upon each other in marriage. Suffocatingly dark in tone, the lyrics seem to have emerged from a John Updike existentialist novel set in upper-crust New England.

A somewhat romantic love song, "The Speed of Love" once again explores the mysterious in between, the place that cannot be identified as tangible but connects a person to a person.

We don't have to talk
We don't even have to touch
I can feel your presence
In the silence that we share

T.S. Eliot inspired "Double Agent," providing the key line, a "wilderness of mirrors" from his 1920 poem "Gerontion," which he had originally hoped to make the prologue to *The Waste Land*, but Ezra Pound fought him on this. With this song, Peart considers the twilight world of indecision and possibilities, when the morals are neither black nor white but immensely and rather terribly grey.

A rocking instrumental, "Leave That Thing Alone," most likely refers to the phallic energy of the first half of the album, followed by an almost country-esque anti-love love song, "Cold Fire," also dealing quite frankly with the strains and nuances of marriage. It is, like many of the lyrics on the album, brutally dark.

The final song, "Everyday Glory," ends the album on a pop-rock note, a song as far removed from the grunge of the opening tracks imaginable. This song would have fit easily on *Presto*, if that album had been written by Bruce Springsteen. The overall atmosphere of the world described is full of anger and corruption, but, Peart writes, a few people will always provide light and goodness for the rest. It is not just their right, but also their very duty to do so.

Nearly thirty years on, *Counterparts* seems shockingly dour in its music and lyrics. It is not surprising that Rush found the album a difficult one to make and considered—perhaps rather seriously for the first time in their history—splitting the band apart.

By the end of the tour, Peart also believed his drumming had reached its highest point possible. This, however, was not good for Peart or for the band. "I felt restless, stagnant, like my playing was getting stiff," he decided, fearing he had traded mathematical precision for poetry.[28] Never content to rest on his own laurels—which would be both immoral as well as boring from Peart's perspective—he decided to relearn how to play the drums. He chose a longtime hero, Freddie Gruber (1927–2011), to retrain him. Gruber taught Peart the theory behind kinetics as much as he taught him technique.

He said, holding up a magisterial finger, "There are no straight lines in nature." Thus our movements should be circular, orbital, smooth and flowing. And, on the drums, we should pay more attention to what happens in the air, between the beats. Another of his finger-raised directives, delivered emphatically, with tall eyes, was, "Get out of the way. Let it happen! Or worse, don't prevent it from happening."[29]

Gruber seems to have been the Socrates of drumming. The iconoclastic Gruber, who had successfully fought a heroin addiction and was the leading drummer of be-bop and big band jazz during the second half of the twentieth century, became not only Peart's closest mentor but a close friend as well. Peart's obituary of the man reveals almost as much about himself as it does of his teacher, Gruber.

As an educator, Freddie's unique gift combined that individual insight with something even greater—he had an unparalleled understanding of the physical "dance" involved in playing the instrument, the ergonomic relationship of the drummer to the drums. That relation was as essential for masters as it was for beginners, and without ever trying to disrupt a particular drummer's "character," he helped each student to discover, express, and refine his own individual voice. His guidance always aimed at a graceful and natural approach to the instrument that was truly musical.[30]

Gruber, Peart claimed, gave him "a different clock."[31] He had nothing but fond things to report about his time with Gruber:

I met Freddie around that same time of the recording of the Buddy Rich tribute. We became lifelong friends and started working together to loosen my playing up and make it a dance. That's what his coaching was all about. It was all physical, not musical. He's not the kind of teacher who teaches you how to play the drums. He teaches you how to dance on the drums. At that time, '95 or so, I'd been playing then for 30 years. "Am I really going to stop now, practise every day with these exercises he's giving me, go back to traditional grip, the right end of the sticks?" Because I'd been playing butt-end with matched grip for a long time by then. He had me moving the snare drum up, the bass drum farther away—so counterintuitive. I always thought, get everything as close as you can and then you have the best reach on it—but in fact no, it's your area of motion. It's better to have your bass drum, toms, ride cymbal a little farther away, so it was completely re-inventing the way I play the instrument.

I had to say, "Can I do it and is it worth it? Can I go down to the basement every day and practise again like I did when I was 13? If I can commit myself to that, will I be rewarded?" I decided it was worth the try and did that for about a year and a half. The band happened not to be working because Geddy and his wife were having a baby so it was perfect timing, such synchronicity, finding Freddie, just the right guy. He really helped me in that way of loosening it all up again within the framework and carrying forward with the accuracy and it was still my playing. A lot of people, even my bandmates, couldn't tell the difference, at first until they played with me and then they noticed the clock was different just from that new physical approach to playing the kit. It was such a subtle approach that our co-producer at the time Peter Collins said, "Well it still sounds like you: I was kind of disappointed but then when the other guys played with me, they noticed that the clock was different, as they do now because I've entered another period that kind of echoes that."[32]

Studying with Gruber gave Peart a satisfied confidence he had not previously known. In his book, *Roadshow*, Peart, who had only one teacher as a teenager, admitted that "no matter how much I practiced and played and showed off, the more praise I received, the more I felt like a hacker, a sham, and a fraud."[33] After having formally been a student, he began to believe he had much to teach. This was, to Peart's way of thinking, a natural part of the process of excellence—the student becoming the professor.[34] Consequently, he has released five instructional and informational drum DVDs: *The Making of Burning for Buddy; A Work in Progress; Anatomy of a Drum Solo; Fire on Ice*; and *Taking Center Stage*. Each reveals a happy, relaxed yet intense, and humorous Peart, sometimes in the studio and sometimes on the road.

After spending time learning with Gruber, Peart then studied with Weather Report's Peter Erskine, a master of jazz fusion.[35]

Still a devoted drumming student, just last year [2009], Peart took lessons from renowned jazz drummer Peter Erskine to expand his percussive palette with daily practices, focusing on the hi-hat and metronome. In fact, it was Erskine who encouraged Peart to loosen up his hi-hat technique.[36]

When the Canadian hockey league asked Peart to rewrite the national hockey theme, he decided it would be the perfect time to apply all of the techniques he had learned from Erskine.[37] He was additionally thrilled by the opportunity to write for the Canadian national sport (one at which he had never been good). He said, "I spent, honestly two months on that one minute of music, refining that part and rehearsing it." He wanted to place everything he knew into that sixty seconds. "It proved well worth doing," he stated. "It was one of the greatest experiences of my life."[38] Tellingly, he noted at the beginning of the project that he wanted to experiment as much and as radically as possible, hoping it would flow into a coherent theme.[39] The song he composed, after all, would essentially become nothing less than a new version of the second national anthem for Canada.

That Peart, already considered by most to be the world's greatest drummer, would decide it was his duty to relearn his craft, to start from the beginning, speaks volumes about the man's drive and his integrity. It also reveals much about his character, all positive. In the best way, Peart never accepted second best.

TEST FOR ECHO

Test for Echo (1996), the band's sixteenth studio album, is an anomaly and a beautiful transition from the second full stage of Rush (2.0) before culminating in Rush (3.0). Arriving a full three years after *Counterparts*, Rush fandom had never had to wait so long for a new album from the band. "During that time," Peart noted in the official tour book, "Geddy and his wife produced a baby girl, Alex produced a solo album [*Victor*], and I produced a tribute to the big-band music of Buddy Rich. We worked; we traveled; we lived our lives; and it was fine."[40] The title of the album even reflects the time away from one another and from their fans. *Test for Echo*, Peart explains, was a means of Rush both asking and assuring its fan base that neither was alone. "Everybody needs an 'echo,' some affirmation to know they're not alone."[41]

Test for Echo possesses neither the overall hardness of the 1993 album, *Counterparts*, nor the denseness of a *Power Windows* (1985). Neither, however, was it as light and sleek as *Presto* (1989) had been. Instead, it sounds like almost nothing Rush had done before, and yet, like nothing Rush has done since. Still, it is thoroughly Rush. In the context of the history of Rush, *Test for Echo* is, to be sure, its own creature. Certainly, Lifeson had never played such a strong and assertive role in the creation of an album as he did with this one. Peter Collins, English producer of *Power Windows* (1985), *Hold Your Fire* (1987), and *Counterparts*, returned to produce this album, keeping his view on the overall structure of the full album, with Clif Norrell (Catherine Wheel) serving as recording engineer and Andy Wallace (Faith No More) as mixing engineer.[42] While *Test for Echo* contains a number of relentlessly driving songs, it also contains a considerable amount of whimsy and humor. Lee explains why the album needed each to best reflect its true meaning: "It's about the numbing process that happens when we are exposed to great tragedies and then we're exposed to moments of hilarity," Lee told a reporter. "I feel that that's the condition of contemporary man now—when we read the paper or when we watch TV, we're not sure if we're supposed to laugh."[43] Despite being the most "progressive" album the band had produced in a decade or so, *Test for Echo* also possesses a relaxed, comfortable feel to it, something rarely found on a Rush album. Strangely, however, the band—especially Lee and Lifeson—felt real tension with one another during the recording of the album. There were, according to Lifeson, even a few explosions at and with one another. Lee remembers the process of making the album with next to no fondness.

Test for Echo *was a strange record in a sense. It doesn't really have a defined direction. I kind of felt like we were a bit burnt creatively. It was a creative low time for us.*[44]

Peart, however, downplayed the tensions, at least in his remembrances, and instead focused on the new drumming technique he had learned from Freddy Gruber between *Counterparts* and this album. "I could feel I had brought my playing to a whole new level, both technically and musically."[45] Indeed, by the following summer, Peart was so enthusiastic about the album and the tour that he claimed "we're already planning our next studio album."[46] In an interview with Eric Deggans of the *St. Petersburg Times*, Peart thought the band had reached its peak. "Over the years, we learned how to write, how to play and how to arrange and now we have a full toolbox. Time and experience ... there's no substitute for that." With previous albums, the drummer claims, he "struggled to find new ways of challenging" himself. But of *Test for Echo* he said, "I came in with so much that I had to edit myself."[47]

After three years of the three members of the band being apart, though, it took more than a bit of time and patience for the band to come back together as a whole. As mentioned above, Lee expressed frustration toward the beginning of the project. "Neil was being Mr. Aloof a little bit. So we kind of circled each other and we talked."[48]

Lifeson also wanted to play a bigger role than usual in making the album. He had learned a great deal writing and producing his solo album, *Victor*, and he hoped to share that knowledge and wisdom with Rush. Previously, however, Lifeson had played a vital but only supporting role when it came to designing the albums. Lee admitted that with *Test for Echo* he and Peart gave Lifeson more room than had been normal. "I think Neil and I relaxed a little bit more and gave Alex some say," he noted. "I think Neil and I can be, um, well I guess we can be pushy."[49]

Whatever the tension, the end result, *Test for Echo*, is a thing of wonder. Beginning with an airy atmosphere and almost pleading guitar, the opening track, the title track, resolves into a progressive grunge. The lyrics express shock at a world that has become completely commodified in the images the media presents to the world. The result, vertigo.

Don't touch that dial—
We're in denial

Lyrically, the song complements "Show Don't Tell" from *Presto*. Yet unlike that deeply personal and self-judgmental song, this one asks how all of what was once private is now public? How did this happen so quickly?

As if Peart has to respond to the intrusion and commercialized weaponization of mass media, he offers a statement of integrity in the following song, "Driven." Unlike earlier Rush songs that deal with similar themes, "Driven" leaves lingering questions. Can a person be so driven that he finds himself "driven to the edge of a deep dark hole"? Yet, Peart (and the listener) avoids the abyss, determined not to linger in any one place too long. "And I go riding on," the song concludes. "Driven" offers Rush at its best: great lyrics; a perfectly progressive rhythm; and Lifeson's tastefully grungy guitar sound. Lee considers it a "quintessential Rush song."[50] During the live performance of "Driven" captured on Rush's triple-live CD *Different Stages*, a fan appropriately yells, "Take it off, Alex," as the guitarist rips through his solo on this song.

The video Rush produced for this song is possibly the most interesting video the band ever made. Visually, it anticipates the grime of *The Matrix*, but it also intertwines elements of *Blade Runner* and the original version of *The Road Warrior*. Armed with measures of the bizarre and carnival-esque, the video is pure punk dystopia, and Lee, playing the role of protagonist, appears to be having the time of his life.

The third song, "Half the World," enters a heavy candy-pop-rock world of music. Lyrically, however, Peart continues to express shock at the state of the world, a world divided by so many things. Some trivial, some major. Taking the lyrics literally, the listener cannot help but believe the world will always remain thus divided. The ultimate division: those who lie and steal; and those who live honorably.

The fourth song, "The Color of Right," offers a more positive take on similar notions, noting that right (and righteousness, properly understood) can transcend all differences in this world. This is Peart at his Platonic and Aristotelian best. Reality exists, but we have the free will to make it beautiful.

Track five, "Time and Motion," returns the listener to the style of the first two tracks of the album, offering nothing less than a mini-prog gem. As the title indicates, the song plays with the modernist ideas of time and movement, similar to "Natural Science" on *Permanent Waves*.

Time and motion
Flesh and blood and fire
Lives connect in webs of gold and razor wire

Everything is connected to everything else in this world, and, yet, this can mean we're each attached to both the good and the ill. Thus, man must be:

Superman in Supernature
Needs all the comfort he can find
Spontaneous emotion
And the long-enduring kind

"Totem" looks, rather whimsically and more than a bit mockingly, at all types of religions, meshing Christianity with Hinduism with a variety of pagan practices. The song ends, ominously, with "Sweet chariot, swing low, coming for me."

"Dog Years," the seventh track, again reveals Rush's rather humorous side and considers exactly what the title claims: the life of a dog, complete with fleas, sniffs, and howls. That this song appears after "Totem" is not accidental. Both explore irrationality and instinct. In ancient Greek, the word for dog is cynic. Whether Peart embraces the romantic or the cynical is open to question on this album.

Peart, however, considered the song a "feast" at the time of its release, arguing at length about its own depths.

Even the story of its writing is kind of amusing, because it was right when we got together for the first time, the three of us, after quite a long break apart. We did a little celebrating the first night and the following day I was a bit the worse for wear, and a little dull-witted, and I thought, "Gee, I don't think I'm going to get much done today, but I'm a professional, I'd better try." So I sat down all muzzy-headed like that and started trying to stitch words together—that's what I was there for, after all. "Dog Years" is what came out of that kind of mentality, and born of observations over the years too, of looking at my dog thinking, "What's going through his brain?" and I would think, "Just a low-level zzzzz static." "Food. Walk." The basic elemental things. When I look at my dog that's how I see his brainwaves moving. Other elements are in there of dog behavior, and I've had this discussion with other dog owners too: "What do you think your dog is really thinking about?" I say, "I don't think he's thinking about too much." That was certainly woven into it as well.[51]*

A heavy track that would not have appeared out of place on *Counterparts*, "Virtuality" considers the reality and unreality of the World Wide Web, connecting all things intangibly, one to another.

"Resist" is a deeply personal anthem, a restatement of Peartian principles of individualism, but done so in a very acoustic, singer-songwriter-friendly way. Inspired by the dark romantic, Oscar Wilde, "Resist" never crosses the line into melodrama.[52] Rather, it successfully embraces a bardic feel. "I can learn to close my eyes/to anything but injustice."

Combining humor with a progressive rhythm, "Limbo," offers an instrumental Rush version of the "Monster Mash," complete with Frankenstein sound effects. Interestingly enough, it's also a play on and against a more controversial Rush, radio personality Rush Limbaugh.[53]

"Carve Away the Stone" finishes the album on an uplifting note, rewriting the tragic Greek myth of Sisyphus. In the traditional story, the gods punish Sisyphus for his deceit, making him roll a stone up a mountain, only to have it roll back down, forcing Sisyphus to start all over again, endlessly. In the ancient version, the gods punish Sisyphus not just for his deceit but also for his hubris, that is, his very challenge of and to the power of the gods. Peart's extremely Stoic lyrics call for the good person to accept the fate of the gods, and to push the stone with all his best effort and integrity, thus showing to the gods and all of humanity that man can indeed best them. The song ends with the wry note: "If you could just move yours/I could get working on my own." In other words, every man, woman, and child shares the fate of Sisyphus in this world. Accept it and move on.

The year 1996 also saw Peart publish his first book, *The Masked Rider: Cycling in West Africa*. As noted previously in this work, Peart had aspired to be a writer—of fiction or nonfiction—for all of his adult life. And he had written quite a bit, but much of it was unconventional, at least by twentieth-century standards. Not only had he written lyrics, he had written a number of articles for various publications. Like all things that Peart decided to approach, he wanted to approach writing with a certain perfection. "Over the years I've developed a stronger and stronger interest in prose writing," he explained in a 1984 interview. "I've pushed myself as a lyricist, just as I did as a drummer, to constantly explore new areas and use different constructions, rhyming patterns, and rhythms."[54]

Equally important, he had—in the nineteenth-century fashion of a Henry Adams—written what one might justly regard as very long essays or relatively short books about his own travels: *Riding the Golden Lion* (1985); *The Orient Express* (1987); *Pedals over the Pyrenees* (1988); *Raindance over the Rockies* (1988); and *The Masked Rider* (1990).[55] He published each of these privately and with distribution limited only to a few friends. As it turned out, the travelogue proved the form in which Peart's writings would best emerge.

> The best part of adventure travel, it seems to me, is thinking about it. A journey to a remote place is exciting to look forward to, certainly rewarding to look back upon, but not always pleasurable to live minute by minute. Reality has a tendency to be so uncomfortably real.[56]

It was this last privately published travelogue that Peart would expand and publish as his first book, using the same title.

Years of practice gave Peart the confidence he needed to publish *The Masked Rider* in 1996. While is it not as polished as his later books, it is truly an astounding book regardless of what one does or does not know of Peart. That is, if I handed the book to a literature professor who possessed no knowledge of the author's background as a drummer, a rock musician, or as a lyricist, he or she would find the book simply ... good. Very good.

In many ways, writing lyrics or writing poetry is something quite different from writing prose at any length. While it is easy to see the poetic elements of well-written prose, it is much more difficult to find the opposite, prose in well-written poetry. Peart does both well, but he does them differently. His lyrics have the feel of philosophy at times and Imagistic poetry at other times. His prose, though, has a definite style, harmonizing the descriptive power of a Willa Cather with the humorous and witty insights of a Jack Kerouac. He also possesses what might be labeled an eidetic memory. Some people possess a photographic memory (as Abraham Lincoln or Russell Kirk did), remembering words and the ordering of words years after having seen them. Famously, students would pull books off Russell Kirk's shelves, ones he had not looked at in decades. When asked what appeared on this or that page, or this or that paragraph on some page, Kirk could recall every word and line, perfectly. Peart seems to have the same talent with things he sees. He can uncannily remember every rock, stream, tree, or building. Or so it seems. It allows him to play (rather serious play, as Plato would have put it) anthropologist, cultural critic, and natural historian to a degree mostly lost in a world of constant flows of information and bombardment of sound and fury in the media. In all of his published books, Peart provides not just impressions, but actual and very interesting details, whether he is writing about the shape of the land, the ways of a people, or the behavior of a species.

What makes *The Masked Rider* so impressive—especially as a first published book for any author—is that Peart writes his travelogue ostensibly about his bicycle trips through West Africa in the late 1980s. What he really does, however, is analyze himself, his traveling companions, the people he encounters, and the situations that arise through the lens of Aristotle's famous work *The Nichomachaen Ethics*. In that great letter to his son, the justly famous Greek posited that merely through the observation of natural events and a recognition of the natural law, one could understand not only the moral good of a thing or a person but that he or she could also judge the behavior and the norms of a community. No omniscient, omnipresent, omnipotent being need exist and no laws needed to be handed to one on stone tablets. Rather, one could discover the ills of immoral behavior as always malicious—sometimes immediately and sometimes gradually—within a society, whatever its scale. In Aristotle's explanation, the highest of all goods is to seek happiness. Happiness, though, is not satiation of appetite, it is satisfaction with human excellence, culminating in the virtues.

Peart had come to these ideas independently of Aristotle, but reading the *Ethics* as he rode through Africa confirmed as well as shattered many of his own personal beliefs. As it would turn out, the year that saw the arrival in the world of *Test for Echo* and *The Masked Rider* would prove the last "normal" year of Peart's life. And far more beliefs than his natural Aristotelianism would take a profound beating. 1997 and 1998 would be years of hell. Pure, unadulterated hell.

---

1. Steffan Chirazi, "Firestarter!" *Kerrang!* (October 3, 1987).
2. Paul Elliot, *Sounds* (October 31, 1987).
3. Peart quoted in Brett Milano, "The Down-To-Earth Rush," *Boston Globe* (November 19, 1987).
4. One can find Peart's most immediate appreciation for Jefferson in his 2014 book, *Far and Near*, 87.
5. Peart offered his most sustained conversation about Aristotle in his first book, *The Masked Rider*. Interestingly enough, he brought Aristotle's *Ethics*

with him on his first bike trip across West Africa, judging himself, one of his fellow bicyclists, Elsa, and the Africans he met by Aristotle's standards. The author makes twenty-one references to the ancient Greek philosopher. The reader can find a fuller description of *The Masked Rider* at the end of chapter three of this book.

6. Paul Elliot, *Hold Your Fire* review, *Sounds* (October 31, 1987).
7. Steffan Chirazi, "Firestarter!," *Kerrang!* (October 3, 1987).
8. Phil Wilding, "The Meaning of Lifeson," *Kerrang!* (November 25, 1989); and "Geddy Lee on Rockline for Presto," *Rockline* (December 4, 1989).
9. William F. Miller, "Interview: Neil Peart/Rush," *Modern Drummer* (December 1989).
10. Imagism was the very first form of modernist poetry, founded by the great humanist and warrior, T.E. Hulme, at the very beginning of the twentieth century. Forsaking traditional verse, beats, and stanzas, Imagism sought to connect all things to a visual. Words themselves served as visuals, literally and symbolically, connecting one thing to another, one idea to another, and one person to another. At its highest, Imagism hoped to unify all things. Though Hulme invented the form, Eliot perfected it, especially in his final four poems, *The Four Quartets*.
11. Steve Streeter, "Life on Paper!" *A Show of Fans* 17 (Summer 1997).
12. William F. Miller, "Neil Peart: In Search of the Right Feel," *Modern Drummer* (February 1994).
13. Peart, *Far and Near*, 245.
14. Peart, *Far and Near*, 242, 245.
15. Interview with Neil Peart by Jim Ladd, *Deep Tracks* (February 3, 2015).
16. Again, a necessary thanks to Steve H. for this observation.
17. Lee quoted in *Beyond the Lighted Stage*.
18. Paglia, *Sexual Personae: Art and Decadence from Nefertiti to Emily Dickinson* (New Haven, CT: Yale University Press, 1990), 2–3.
19. Paglia, *Sex, Art, and American Culture*, 108.
20. Paglia, *Sex, Art, and American Culture*, 106.
21. Paglia, *Sex, Art, and American Culture*, 117. It is more than likely that Peart's fascination and appreciation for Madonna came from Paglia as well as from his second wife, Carrie Nuttall. See Peart, *Traveling Music*, 270–271.
22. Paglia, *Sexual Personae*, 1.
23. Paglia, *Sexual Personae*, 8.
24. Paglia, *Sexual Personae*, 14.
25. Peart quoted in Jim DeRogatis, "Progressive Thinking Gives Rush New Life," *Chicago Sun Times* (March 27, 1994).
26. Jim DeRogatis, "Rush Reconsidered," *Request* (January 1994). See also, Tony Green, "In No Hurry to Change," *St. Petersburg Times* (March 4, 1994).
27. Arjen Lucassen, quoted in Malcom Dome, "Rush: R40," *Prog* 52 (January 2015): 45.
28. Christine M. Cooney, "Peart Interview," *Connecticut Post* (November 8, 1996).
29. Peart, *Traveling Music*, 33.
30. Neil Peart, "In Memorium: Freddie Gruber," hudsonmusic.com (October 12, 2011).

31. Andy Greene, "Q&A: Neil Peart On Rush's New LP And Being A 'Bleeding Heart Libertarian,'" *Rolling Stone* (June 12, 2012).
32. David West, "Close Up on Neil Peart," *Rhythm* (August 2011).
33. Peart, *Roadshow*, 84–84.
34. Christine M. Cooney, "Peart Interview," *Connecticut Post* (November 8, 1996).
35. David E. Libman, "Neil Peart: Master Class," *Drum!* (October 2012).
36. "Neil Peart Interview," *Guitar Center* (February 2010).
37. Neil Peart, "Fire on Ice," liner notes (Drum Channel, 2010).
38. Dave Feschuk, "Hockey Anthem a Rush," *Toronto Star* (January 14, 2010).
39. Neil Peart, in conversation, "Fire on Ice: The Making of 'The Hockey Theme,'" (Drum Channel DVD, 2010).
40. Peart, *The Test for Echo Tour Book: Official Guidebook and User's Manual* (1996).
41. Peart, *Test for Echo Tour Book*.
42. Peart, *Test for Echo Tour Book*.
43. Lee quoted in Jim Abbott, "Echo Has More than One Meaning," *Minneapolis Star Tribune*, October 27, 1996.
44. Lee quoted in Vinay Menon, *Rush: An Oral History, Uncensored*. At the time of the album release, Lifeson felt great about it. See his interview with Steven Batten, "Testing for Echo: Rush Return After Two Years in Hiding," *Northeast Ohio Scene* (October 31–November 6, 1996). Lifeson especially liked the "aggressiveness" of his guitar. Peart thought that the tension came from Lifeson, as he had the experience of producing *Victor* on his own and wanted to assert much of what he'd learned from that. See Alan Sculley, "Rushing Back Into the Spotlight," *St. Louis Post-Dispatch*, June 5, 1997.
45. Peart, *Traveling Music*, 34.
46. Peart quoted in Betsy Powell, "Peart is a Different Drummer," *Toronto Star*, June 30, 1997, pg. E4.
47. Peart quoted in Eric Deggans, "Rush Recharged," *St. Petersburg Times*, December 6, 1996, pg. 18.
48. Lee interview, "Test for Echo World Premier," WKSC-FM (Chicago), September 5, 1996.
49. Lee quoted in Katherine Monk, "What a Rush," *Vancouver Sun*, May 15, 1997, pg. C1.
50. Lee interview, "Test for Echo World Premier," WKSC-FM (Chicago), September 5, 1996.
51. Peart, "Test for Echo World Premier," WKSC-FM, September 5, 1996.
52. Peart, *Test for Echo Tour Book*.
53. Paul Verna, "After a 3-Year Break, Trio Regroups for New Atlantic Set," *Billboard* (August 3, 1996).
54. Budofsky, *Modern Drummer Legends: Rush's Neil Peart*, 20.
55. Peart's travels in Africa also led to one of his finest collaborations with Kevin J. Anderson, "Drumbeats," a gloriously creep tale of the weird. See Anderson/Peart, *Drumbeats: Special Edition* (Monument, CO: WordFire Press, 2020).
56. Peart, *The Masked Rider*, xii.

4 REBIRTH, RENAISSANCE, AND THE END
1997–2020

During the evening of August 10, 1997, a police car pulled up to Peart's house to inform him and his wife, Jackie, that their only child, nineteen-year-old Selena, had been killed in an automobile accident that day.[1] Unable to bear the tragedy, Jackie collapsed, internally and externally. Peart did as well, but he also possessed a much stronger constitution than did his wife. Strangely, as Peart notes so effectively in his best book, *Ghost Rider*, most couples who lose a child never heal, their relationship doomed to collapse. "So wrong, so unfair, so cruel, to heap more pain and injustice on those who had suffered so much already," he cries.[2] Jackie took her grief out on Peart as well as on herself. "She no longer wanted anything," he remembers, "she just wanted to die."[3] Indeed, she thought her own death would serve as a kind of justice for failing to protect her daughter from harm as a mother ideally should. Again, though less destructive than Jackie, Peart sought solace in "a numb refuge of alcohol and drugs."[4] Less than a year after Selena's death, decimated by cancer diagnosed too late to stop, Jackie passed away.[5] How to deal with this double tragedy plagued Peart, a shattered soul.

I didn't really have a reason to carry on; I had no interest in life, work, or the world beyond, but unlike Jackie, who had surely willed her death, I seemed to be armored with some kind of survival instinct, some inner reflex that held to the conviction that "something will come up." Because of some strength (or flaw) of character, I never seemed to question "why" I should survive, but only "how"—though that was certainly a big enough question to deal with at the time.[6]

During the days after Selena's death, Lifeson and Lee stayed with the grieving couple, trying to provide company and sympathy.[7] Naturally concerned, Lifeson and Lee felt at a loss, not knowing how to help but offering him all they could. "Neil was completely lost," Lifeson exclaimed. "We all were. It's amazing how much dies in you at such a time, and how vulnerable you can feel."[8] Peart quietly informed his bandmates he was resigning from Rush.

"We put any thought of Rush's future away. In some sense we believed it probably was over," Lee said in 2002.[9] His bandmates removed even the semblance of pressure to make music from Peart, offering only their support.[10]

"I don't think he'll be the person he was," Lifeson told a reporter, "but I think he will cope with life again."[11]

Protecting what little he had left of his very being after the loss of his wife and daughter, a tragic and despondent Peart climbed on his motorcycle and began to ride. And ride. And, ride. He did so for nearly 14 months, traveling throughout all of North America on what he called "The Healing Road." During his travels, Peart slowly began to find himself, understanding that his past was over, his old existence over, and whatever life remained to be reborn. He called this an "existential discomfort."[12] On this journey, his new holy trinity, as he put it, became "landscapes, highways, and wildlife."[13] In his fourteen-month self-imposed exile, he rode 55,000 miles.

In his bestselling book, *Ghost Rider*, Peart not only proves to be an excellent writer (imagine Willa Cather and Jack Kerouac as one person; a bizarre combination, I know, but an accurate one, as discussed in the previous chapter), but he also reveals himself, yet again, a serious and Stoic social and cultural critic. Here are two sample passages from *Ghost Rider*.

The first day in Mexico was Selena's birthday, and I had made careful plans on how to "memorialize" that day. Early in the morning, I walked to the big cathedral in the Zocalo, went inside and bought two princess-sized votive candles (the biggest they had, of course) and lit them in front of the chapel for "Nuestra Señora de Guadalupe...." I sat there awhile, and cried some (well, a lot), amid the pious old ladies, tourists, and construction workers.[14]

Later in the book, in a less autobiographical nature, he explains his own vision of what art is.

I once defined the basic nature of art as "the telling of stories," and never had I felt that to be more true. I played the anger, the frustration, the sorrow, and even the travelling parts of my story, the rhythms of the highway, the majesty of the scenery, the dynamic rising and falling of my moods, and the narrative suite that emerged was as cleansing and energizing as the sweat and exertion of telling it.[15]

Each of these passages shows Peart at his deepest: the side of him that craves beauty and the side of him that craves telling the world about the beauty he has seen.

His travels also opened Peart to a number of personal revelations. Overall, he believed that "the elemental 'faith' in life I used to possess is completely gone," and that with such an erasing of the past and its securities, "every little element of my former life, behavior, interests, and habits, was up for re-examination."[16] Two specifics also emerged in this rebirth. First, he had to accept the help of others, recognizing it as the gift it is and was intended to be by the giver. Pride had to give way to charity. Second, he came to see a more mystical side of life, well beyond his previously steady devotion to late eighteenth-century European rationalism. In one incident—that would greatly influence the next three albums—Peart encountered a man who read his fortune through tarot cards. The reading proved so accurate that Peart's "jaw dropped, and it's still dropping."[17]

Though most orthodox religions forbid the reading of tarot, artists as diverse as T.S. Eliot and Russell Kirk have employed its meaning—however tragic and deep or superficial and meaningless—effectively as a form of storytelling, especially regarding character and morals. Peart does the same through his lyrics over the next several albums.

His revelations, his travels, his eye-opening encounters all led to a profound healing for Peart. None of these tragedies ever disappeared for Peart, of course, nor should they have. They pained him for the rest of his days on this earth.[18] Still, after his terrible struggles and his wrestling with the demons of this world, he came to accept his losses in Stoic fashion. Critically and vitally, he fell in love again, this time with famed photographer Carrie Nuttall, daughter of well-respected history professor, Donald Nuttall (Whittier College, now passed away).[19] For all intents and purposes, love saved him.

If there is anything worse in normal life than losing one's child, I have not discovered it. It is, simply, unnatural. On August 8, 2007, my wife and I lost our own child, Cecilia Rose. My wife had come to full term with her pregnancy on August 6, and we decided to wait rather than induce. As it turns out, our judgment proved fatal. Sometime on the morning of August 8, my wife felt a horrific jolt in her stomach. Misunderstanding the movement as a strange contraction we went to the hospital. Somehow, our Cecilia had become strangled by her umbilical cord. The very thing that nourished her, killed her. Having discovered this, my wife and I had to wait for another sixteen or so hours for her to deliver a dead baby girl. My wife delivered the baby with all of the grace and strength imaginable. For a few moments, Cecilia Rose remained warm, still heated by her mother's womb, but she quickly cooled as we held her and beheld her, a body whole but soulless.

While we never knew our Cecilia Rose in way that Neil Peart knew his daughter Selena as a complete and beautiful personality, the loss of a child—at any age—is a horror of horrors. Every August 8, no matter the warmth or sun of the day, a depression sets upon us both, and I'm sure it will for the remainder of our days on this earth. I wonder what that little princess would have done, how many boys she would've inspired to slay dragons. Neil Peart, I am sure, wondered how much his Selena would've done as a doctor or an artist or a writer or a professor … All questions that will never be answered no matter how many other joys enter a life. There simply is no replacing any single one of us.

I first read *Ghost Rider* after the loss of our own Cecilia Rose. As with everything else Peart has written since 1981, *Ghost Rider* helped me break out of my own depression and avoid foolish decisions that would have, ultimately, proved disastrous for my family. Peart gave me words when necessary ones simply were unavailable around me. He did that for me when I was in seventh-grade detention at age thirteen, and he did the same for me while suffering through a family tragedy at the age of 39.

It would not be an exaggeration to argue that meeting Carrie was one of the most important moments in Peart's life and helped to precipitate Rush 3.0. In her, Peart found a reason to live fully, a reason to rediscover excellence, and a reason to return to his life in Rush. It was through their mutual friend, Andrew McNaughton (now deceased), that the two met.

> *In those days, Andrew and I often talked on the phone from wherever I wandered, and shared our sorrows and anxieties. Typically, Andrew was determined to find a "match" for this crusty old widower. When my motorcycle had carried me back across the continent yet again, to pause in Halifax, Nova Scotia, Andrew sent me a few test Polaroids of a photo assistant he had been working with—a pretty dark-haired girl named Carrie. Again, I was reluctant, gruffly telling him, "not interested"—but finally I made my meandering way west again, and stopped for a while in Los Angeles.*[20]

When she met Peart, she knew next to nothing about the band.[21] She told him, however, that she would love to see him perform again, especially considering his reputation as a drummer and his own love of music. For Peart, all of this proved almost Faerie-like.

> *Andrew introduced me to Carrie, my real angel of redemption; in less than a month we were deeply in love, and in less than a year we were married in a fairy-tale wedding near Santa Barbara. Carrie: Beautiful, smart, cultivated, artistic, affectionate; Deep green eyes, long dark hair, radiant smile; Tall, slender, shapely, nicely put together; Half English, half Swedish, all American, all mine. The answer to a prayer I hadn't dared to voice, or even dream. Carrie. A friend, a soulmate, a lover, a wife, a new journey to embark upon, the greatest adventure.*[22]

Though still in pain—a pain that would never fully cease—when he met her, he found her instantly attractive intellectually as well as personally. They bonded almost immediately in friendship. She considered him a modern-day Conquistador, armed in black leather and mounted on a powerful red horse, forever seeking the road and adventure. But his days of restless exploration had come to an end, and the Ghost Rider faded into memory. On September 9, 2000, just three days short of his forty-eighth birthday, Peart married Nuttall in Montecito, California.[23]

Ever since they met, Peart demonstrated a sheer joy in his

writing—not only how he wrote but what he wrote—that is lacking in his pre-2000 writings. Part of the explanation might simply be age and wisdom, but Peart made Carrie a part of his public life in ways he never had with Jackie. Of course, this might have been Jackie's choice as well. Regardless, Peart was especially happy when Carrie became an immediate part of his Rush life. Not atypically, Peart gushes about her visit to a concert.

> Carrie flew into Nashville for the last few days of rehearsal and the first show, and out of deference to Her Ladyship, Michael and I moved to a slightly nicer—or at least more central—hotel. Before Carrie and I met, in 1999, all she knew about the band was a teenage memory of hearing "Tom Sawyer" or "The Spirit of Radio" on car radios, but she liked to watch our shows. At the Nashville rehearsal hall, she put in her earplugs and joined the small audience sitting in a handful of chairs in the middle of the dark, booming soundstage, and watched us go through the show. I liked being able to look out and see her there, my pre-Raphaelite beauty giving me a smile and a wave.[24]

Mixing her own profession with his, Nuttall published a gorgeous and artful book of photography, *Rhythm & Light* (Rounder, 2005), all of it dealing with her husband's drumming. The project began when the two missed one another because of their respective professional commitments as Rush began writing *Vapor Trails*. The two agreed that he would be her next project.

"Well known for his private and sometimes reclusive nature, Neil had never before allowed anyone—friend, family member or photographer—to be privy to the day-to-day process of his creative life."[25]

Though he balked a bit at first, Peart found he loved the togetherness as well as his wife's art. Indeed, he gave her complete access to his re-learning of the drums and his interactions with the entire Rush team.

As she put it, he put all his vanity aside. "I was surprised to note the quiet elegance, grace, and refinement that was evident, along with the more expected raw, powerful, intense energy associated with rock drumming," she explained.[26] She already knew of her husband's intensity, but seeing him in action actually shocked her.

"I always knew he was focused," Nuttall said, "but I had never seen him in the role of drummer and lyricist before we got married. And I wasn't prepared for it. You hear stories, but until you've seen it firsthand, you have no idea. And that's what it was with me seeing Neil take on those roles."[27]

The end product, *Rhythm & Light*, pleased Peart greatly. "Both Carrie and her subject are caught here in the purity of that pursuit," he reflected. "Hers for the light, his for the rhythm."[28]

However much happiness his wife and daughter, Olivia Louise (b. 2009) brought the Canadian drummer, writer, and lyricist—and that happiness is immense—the scars, understandably, remained.

The scars remain tender. Never, ever healed, but only lightly scabbed over. Time does not heal all wounds, but only allows us to adapt, if we can, to a life that is forever altered. Some wounds are like physical disabilities that will never heal, but can only be compensated for, adapted to. Now when I think back to the dark years of the late '90s, I feel far away in time, even unto building a new life and new memories, and my Ghost Rider persona seems ever more distant—unknowable. I have come to think of that book's author in the third person—another character in another life. Sometimes I feel the way Robert Pirsig portrays his memories of the man he was before electro-convulsive therapy in Zen and the Art of Motorcycle Maintenance.[29]

If all art is the telling of a story, Peart continued his in what I refer to as Rush 3.0.

Not only did Peart lose and rediscover himself, he had to do the same with the drums when he returned to work in 2001. "The first day we started work on the album, Neil was driving into Toronto from Quebec. He said that the closer he got to Toronto the more grey and foreboding the skies got, and the more he felt like turning back."[30]

Lifeson wondered if the band could recover its skills. He especially wondered if Peart would recover his skills:

You could hear him during those early days warming up and it was like, "Oh my God, this is not the drummer that we used to know." And he knew it. He had only played his drums once since the tragedies. It was a long, hard trip back from nothing to build up his stamina and strength.[31]

Slowly, however, Peart began to grow in confidence as the three began to rehearse together, getting ready for the album that would be *Vapor Trails*. "For the first three or four weeks back together, we did much more talking than playing," Lee explained. In fact, he thought, they sounded pretty bad at first try.[32] Lifeson and Lee gave Neil his own rooms to write and to practice, thus relieving him of any pressure. "We realized there was a return of spirit happening," Lee noted. "We were pretty focused on making something great."[33] He continues, "we were desperate to prove to each other that we could still rock."[34] As Peart's confidence grew, so did his spirit and so did the spirit of Rush.

Lifeson especially found himself getting emotional as he realized how much life was returning to Peart and to the band.[35] "I think this was a very therapeutic thing for him to do. When he began, he hadn't played in four years, other than a short period in the middle—and this is one of the best drummers in the world!" says Lifeson. "To not play for that long was very difficult. But, you know, music is all about spirit and celebration and the spirit had left us all, especially him. You could see the rejuvenation in him as his playing got better and better. He became more confident. He plays great on this record."[36] Lifeson felt a thrill about the fire they'd rediscovered. "I love that it captured that spark, and I think that's one of the reasons that this record sounds as spirited as it does and as passionate as it does," the guitarist said. "It's pure playing, without too much of your brain getting in the way, which with Rush, in the past, can be a bit of a problem."[37]

With Rush 3.0 came great security and satisfaction in the band. As Lee explained in a deep reminiscence, these were the best years of Rush. When an interviewer asked him about the happiest phase of the band, Lee replied:

I've never thought it like that before, but I can tell you that ever since we came back after Neil's terrible tragedy with his family, and having had those five dark years we were away, every tour I did with Rush I savoured. I would say that period from coming back after Neil's tragedy to the very end were really the golden years for me. I felt like I appreciated every gig, every note that we played. The camaraderie that the three of us had, I never took it for granted, not one day. So I would say that was my happiest time in Rush.[38]

VAPOR TRAILS

Rush released their seventeenth studio album, *Vapor Trails*, on May 14, 2002. Not surprisingly, the emotional tone of the lyrics reflects Peart's life of the previous half decade. The opening track begins, tellingly, with Peart pounding the drums and continues at a throbbing and frantic pace throughout the track. This is truly "One Little Victory," a celebration of life over death.

Celebrate the moment
As it turns into one more
Another chance at victory
Another chance to score

*The measure of the moment
Is a difference of degree
Just one little victory
A spirit breaking free
One little victory
The greatest act can be
One little victory*

Track two, "Ceiling Unlimited," is another blistering track, harder than anything Rush had done in almost a decade. Filled with hope, Peart notes that one can rise above the inanities of the day, a theme he has explored in many previous songs, such as "Tom Sawyer" and "Subdivisions."

*Feeling unlimited
Eyes on the prize
Changes never end
Winding like an ancient river
The time is now again
Hope is like an endless river
The time is now again*

In more pedestrian words, the individual person can achieve almost anything she or he imagines and then some.

"Ghost Rider," the third track, is one of resignation and penance. In this song, the lyricist reflects on his journey into the wilderness, his relentless pursuit of escape after the twin tragedies in his family.

*Pack up all those phantoms
Shoulder that invisible load
Keep on riding north and west
Haunting that wilderness road
Like a ghost rider*

"He really was the Ghost Rider. His recovery was very painful," Lifeson reported at the time. "We spent more time mixing that song than we did recording our first two albums." Yes, the song was that important to the band and to Peart.[39]

Sounding a bit like a latter-day Yes song, "Peaceable Kingdom" wishes what might be true—a Quaker-esque world in which the various peoples of the world love one another.

Dream of a Peaceable Kingdom
Dream of a time without war
The ones we wish would hear us
Have heard it all before

Playfully, Peart inserts a number of images from the tarot, such as "Justice" and "The Hangman."

The following pair of songs, "The Stars Look Down" and "How It Is" consider the notions of fate, acceptance, and resignation. "Have you lived a lifetime today," he asks, "Or do you feel like you just got carried away?" The former song especially posits an omniscient but uncaring god—one who allows the most terrible of tragedies to occur with nothing but a shrug of his shoulders.

Melancholic to the extreme, "Vapor Trail" ponders the fleeting and ephemeral nature of many of the things we consider most important in the world. "Secret Touch" posits Stoic fortitude within the cycles of the world, with Peart's lyrics reflecting those of the very first philosopher in world history, Heraclitus.

The way out
Is the way in
The way out
Is the way in …

One of the most beautiful songs Rush has ever written and produced, "Earthshine" simply rocks.[40] A play on Renaissance science, it offers a glimpse of pure beauty, much in the vein of *Hold Your Fire*'s "Tai-Shan," lyrically.

Earthshine
Stretching out your hand
Full of starlit diamonds
Earthshine
Reflected light
To another's sight
And the moon tells a lover's story
My borrowed face
And my third-hand grace
Only reflect your glory
You're still out of reach
Form a dream to rise to
Earthshine

Following the same trajectory as "Earthshine," "Sweet Miracle" wonders at the unbought grace of life.

Somewhat mercurially, Peart and Co. change direction with "Nocturne" and "Freeze" (Part IV of Fear), each a meditation on unworthiness.

The final track, though, takes us back to the beginning with yet another victory. "Out of the Cradle" is nothing if not a pronouncement that Geddy, Alex, and Neil are back, reborn, renewed, refreshed, and reformed.

It's a dream for the waking
It's a flower touched by flame
It's a gift for the giving
It's a power with a hundred names
Surge of energy, spark of inspiration
The breath of love is electricity
Maybe Time is bird in flight
Endlessly mocking

Here we come out of the cradle
Endlessly rocking
Endlessly rocking

If anything, the 2013 re-mixed version of *Vapor Trails* only highlights Peart's very personal and confessional lyrics. Indeed, if *Grace Under Pressure* examines the state of the world and laments, *Vapor Trails* examines the state of the soul and rejoices ... mostly.

In a move somewhat unusual, Peart openly revealed all of the inspirations for the album in an official press release. It is certainly worth repeating here:

"Lyrically, no overall concept emerged, but I can trace some interesting sources for particular lines," he said.

He said Walt Whitman (liglobal.com/walt/poetry.shtml) influenced the song "Out Of The Cradle," while Thomas Wolfe (www.thomaswolfe.org) inspired "How It Is" and "Ceiling Unlimited."

"Wolfe's title 'Of Time and the River' and looking at a map of the Mississippi Delta suggested the 'winding like an ancient river' lines," Peart said.

"'Ceiling Unlimited' also offers a playful take on Oscar Wilde's reversal of the Victorian lament, 'drink is the curse of the working class,' while Joseph Conrad's 'Victory' gave the 'secret touch on the heart' line."

W.H. Auden and Edward Abbey's "Black Sun" influenced parts of the song "Vapor Trails," Peart said.

Both "Nocturne" and "Secret Touch" were inspired by an article in the Utne Reader called "What Do Dreams Want."

"I was also struck by a psychologist's approach to analysis and dream interpretation, 'without memory or desire,'" he said.

Author A.J. Cronin's 1935 novel title "The Stars Look Down" "seemed to express a fitting view of an uncaring universe," Peart commented. But he took some inspiration from paintings, as well.

Guitarist Alex Lifeson previously told JAM! Music that "Peaceable Kingdom" was originally intended as an instrumental piece, but after the Sept. 11 attacks in New York, it morphed into a meditation on the attacks.

Peart adds that the 19th century Quaker folk artist Edward Hicks "painted no less than 60 versions of the same biblical scene, 'Peaceable Kingdom,' and the tarot card 'The Tower' seemed a chilling reflection of the events of September 11, 2001." (A number of tarot cards are used to illustrate the lyrics on Vapor Trails.*)*

When it came to find a title for the album, Peart said the decision was straightforward.

"A unifying theme sometimes appears in the collected songs and suggests an overall title, like Counterparts *or* Power Windows; *other times a particular song seems emblematic, like 'Test For Echo' or 'Roll The Bones.' Neither approach seemed right this time, so we went with the song title we liked the best, 'Vapor Trail,' and made it plural to refer to all the songs."*[41]

While almost everyone in the music world applauded the return of Peart, after his tragedies, reviewers continued to remain skeptical about the music Rush made. *Rolling Stone,* far less nasty than usual, more or less dismissed *Vapor Trails* as the same as ever when it comes to Rush, but without the complexity of prog.[42] *Rolling Stone* has never embraced prog, but its criticisms were not meant to be complimentary. *Guitar World* gave the album a perplexing 3.5/5 rating without explaining a single negative thing about it.⁴³ Andrew Tuttle of the *Orange County Register* gave the album an A–, claiming that the band had successfully combined all of their previous incarnations while also "explor[ing] adventurous territory."⁴⁴ *Billboard* labeled the album "an absolute triumph."⁴⁵

It must be noted, however, and understandably, that Peart can barely reflect for any length of time on that period of his life.

It was more necessary than anything. That album was just something we had to get through. The Ghost Rider *book is something I'll never read again. They asked me to do an audio version of it and I said, "No." They sent me auditions of other people reading it and I'd get up to about the fourth paragraph and say, "I don't want to listen to this anymore." It was just something that needed to be released and exorcised. That's the way I feel about that album too.*⁴⁶

In his 2011 book *Far and Away*, he admitted:

Listening to some of that music just before setting out on this journey, as the three of us reviewed a couple of remixes of songs from **Vapor Trails** *for an upcoming anthology, I can still sense my emotional state then — an underlying mood of anger and confusion that comes through even in my drumming, never mind the lyrics. I still have the anger, all right, but I think I've left the confusion behind.*⁴⁷

Yet, out of the horrors of Peart's life, renewal came, and powerfully so. The first show of the *Vapor Trails* Tour was in Hartford, Connecticut, June 28, 2002. The three members of Rush — and all of the road crew — experienced tangible anxiety that night. Had they their lost their way? Had they lost their abilities? No, of course not. Rush, that night, became not just Rush, but RushPlus, Rush 3.0. "I remember looking out at the audience and there were people crying," Lifeson remembers of that magical night. "It was so emotional. I guess it was their chance to purge some of their emotions."[48] After the performance—one of the most glorious returns in the history of music—the three men did something they had never done before. They hugged for nearly 10 minutes.[49]

SNAKES AND ARROWS

Snakes and Arrows, Rush's eighteenth studio album, came out on May 1, 2007. It was the last Rush album to be distributed by Atlantic, but the first to be produced by Nick Raskulinecz. *Snake and Arrows* was profoundly progressive, but it was, paradoxically, also one of Rush's bluesiest albums, almost certainly influenced by their EP, *Feedback*, a thirtieth anniversary tribute to the bands the three members loved in the 1960s. And yet, even the blues on the album is mischievous, an inversion or twisting of blues, propelling the flow into more classical progressive directions.

The album also sees the return of Peart, the cultural critic and observer. The first track, "Far Cry," begins with the harrowing "Pariah dogs and wandering madmen," a commentary about the evil in society and those who would sell their own souls and become evil to destroy the other evil. Each, tellingly, is a fundamentalist, "speaking in tongues." The track begins, musically, with a psychedelic blues feel. This was not the world we thought we would inherit, Peart laments.

It's a far cry from the world we thought we'd inherit
It's a far cry from the way we thought we'd share it
You can almost feel the current flowing
You can almost see the circuits blowing

Even when we feel we might actually make something right, the world spins and we find ourselves rolled over.

Track Two, "Armor and Sword," considers what we might do

to protect ourselves and the ones we love from the insanities of the world. Little, it seems.

Confused alarms of struggle and flight
Blood is drained of color
By the flashes of artillery light
No one gets to their heaven without a fight
The battle flags are flown
At the feet of a god unknown
No one gets to their heaven without a fight
Sometimes the damage is too great
Or the will is too weak
What should have been our armor
Becomes a sharp and burning sword

Even when we diagnose our problem and attempt to correct it, we mistake our defense for our offense.

Taken from observations Peart had regarding an older, married couple, "Workin' Them Angels," track three of the album, considers the grace of life, the things that go well when we definitely deserve such help.

All my life
I've been workin' them angels overtime
Riding and driving and living
So close to the edge
Workin' them angels — Overtime
Riding through the Range of Light to the wounded city
Filling my spirit with the wildest wish to fly
Taking the high road to the wounded city
Memory strumming at the heart of a moving picture

Using the same title as a chapter from his memoirs of his bicycle trip across West Africa, *The Masked Rider*, Peart reflects on justice and injustice in the fourth track, "The Larger Bowl." Why does one person have so much while another has nothing? Why does one do little but find everything he needs to live well, while another works his entire life but experiences disaster after disaster? "It's somehow so badly arranged," he laments.

These first four songs really serve as a prelude to the album that is *Snakes and Arrows*, as track five, "Spindrift," begins a relentless journey of majesty until track thirteen, "We Hold On." If there's a flaw in any of these nine tracks, this author has missed them. Peart earns his natural historian hat as he considers the natural phenomenon of "spindrift," the lyrics matching the music perfectly—haunting, swirling, and mesmerizing.

As the waves crash in
On the western shore
It makes me feel uneasy
The spray that's torn away
Is an image of the way I feel

The same happens with relationships, too. "What am I supposed to say?" the lyricist pleads. "Where are the words to answer you, when you talk that way?"

After a rocking instrumental, "The Main Monkey Business," the lyrics return with "The Way the Wind Blows" and the listener experiences the perfect inversion of the traditional blues rock song. With a title harkening back to Bob Dylan, the song begins with a standard blues rock guitar progression. At forty-five seconds into the song, the rhythm changes completely, and the track becomes a swirling mass of prog and, frankly, beautiful, driving confusion, but complete with a refrain that might have come from a Crosby, Stills, and Nash protest song, circa 1968. In many ways, "The Way the Wind Blows" is Rush's finest statement of purpose in their four decades of existence. Lyrically, it mocks those who would allow the times and the spirit of the times—especially if fundamentalist and anti-rationalist—to sweep over them and to shape their fate.

Now it's come to this
Hollow speeches of mass deception
From the Middle East to the Middle West
Like crusaders in unholy alliance
Now it's come to this
Like we're back in the Dark Ages
From the Middle East to the Middle West
It's a plague that resists all science
It seems to leave them partly blind
And they leave no child behind
While evil spirits haunt their sleep
While shepherds bless and count their sheep

Again, as if to tweak the band's critics, an instrumental—"Hope"—comes after "The Way the Wind Blows," followed by Peart's updated version of "Free Will," "Faithless."

I don't have faith in faith
I don't believe in belief
You can call me faithless
But I still cling to hope
And I believe in love
And that's faith enough for me

The song is a paean to individualism and freedom of rational decision-making.

Track ten, "Bravest Face," embraces even the smallest things of life, while also recognizing—much like "Lock and Key" (1987)—that each person has a number of levels to his or her emotional desires and the manifested will. Lifeson's guitar blazes with blues riffs.

Track eleven, "Good News First," adamantly challenges one

of Ayn Rand's most important philosophical concepts, the premise of the "benevolent universe."

The best we can agree on
Is it could have been worse
What happened to your old
"Benevolent universe"
You know the one with stars
That revolve around you
Beaming down full of promises
To bring good news

As if to put an exclamation point on the previous song, thus challenging Rand's egoism, Rush follows it with a brief instrumental entitled "Malignant Narcissism."

The final track, "We Hold On," once again offers a Stoic determinism. How many times, it asks, are we ready to give up, to surrender, and to flee. Winston Churchill supposedly once claimed that if you're going through hell, make sure you keep going. This is Peart's sentiment as well.

Keep going until dawn
How many times must another line be drawn
We could be down and gone
But we hold on

While the press had come to love Rush after Peart's tragedies, and a multitude of stories about the band appeared almost everywhere throughout the media, very few sources actually reviewed *Snakes and Arrows*. Nastily, *Rolling Stone* gave the album three out of five stars, claiming "If you're a Rush fan, add two stars; if not, subtract two."[50] In contrast, their old British stalwart, Geoff Barton, proclaimed the album glorious. "The masters are back. They have assumed control."[51]

CLOCKWORK ANGELS

Rush's nineteenth and last studio album, *Clockwork Angels*, came out on June 12, 2012. It was the only studio album to be distributed by heavy metal label, Roadrunner, and the second to be produced by Nick Raskulinecz. As mentioned at the beginning of this book, the story of *Clockwork Angels* is such an artistic success—as a story, a concert, a novel, a sequel to the novel, a graphic novel, an audiobook, and a series of comic books—that it really overshadows not only the actual album but much of Rush's other art. It is, of course, the culmination of forty years of care, of love, and of purpose. However much the Clockwork universe has dwarfed the album itself, it is very much worth considering the original source material.

Clockwork Angels came out a full six years after *Snakes and Arrows*, a break between albums even greater than that between *Test for Echo* and *Vapor Trails*. Still, few worried as hints came out frequently about the forthcoming Rush album during that time, and Rush even released versions of the two opening songs as singles, performing them on the *Time Machine Tour* of 2011. As few would disagree, the wait for the final product was well worth it. While *Moving Pictures*—because of its time and place in history—might always remain the iconic Rush album, *Clockwork Angels* is arguably the best, cohesive piece of art the band has ever made. It reveals a maturity in lyrics and music understandably absent in the first few Rush albums, but it also possesses every explosion of energy those albums expressed. The band was quite happy with it. "I'm very proud of that record," Lee said in 2015. "It's certainly among our top three pieces of work."[52]

Still, the *Clockwork Angels* story could never have been written by a young man. Tellingly, the novel begins with a grandfather remembering his life. Rush have become, simply put, the elder statesmen of the rock world, a fact finally confirmed by the Cleveland Rock and Roll Hall of Fame in 2013 in its induction ceremony of the band.

Train bells and hydraulic engines establish a steampunk atmosphere—a future based on steam and chemicals rather than electronics—in the opening moments of the first track, "Caravan." This atmosphere quickly dissipates and heavy (I mean, *heavy*) guitar and bass take over, with Lee's wailing voice imitating that of a conductor—welcoming us to new vistas, new ideas, and new worlds. "I can't stop thinking big," repeats Lee. Whatever life has provided in the security of a small, ordered village, the protagonist—whom we later learn is Owen Hardy—needs to explore a world beyond that of his family. "On my way at last, on my way at last," Hardy thinks as he departs from his ancestral home.

On a road lit only by fire
Going where I want, instead of where I should
I peer out at the passing shadows
Carried through the night into the city
Where a young man has a chance of making good
A chance to break from the past

Though "lit only by fire" probably refers to William Manchester's controversial story of the same title, Peart's story deals with an alchemical world, not a specifically medieval one (per Manchester).

With no break in sound, track two, "BU2B," begins. Like "Freewill" and "Faithless," this song deals, in a faerie story-like way, with the huge questions of predestination and free will. Whatever freedom the individual will has, its religious, cultural, ethnic, and linguistic traditions delimit our choices, and we must decide whether to accept the teachings and inheritance of our parents, reject those teachings, or reform them.

I was brought up to believe
The universe has a plan
We are only human
It's not ours to understand
The universe has a plan
All is for the best
Some will be rewarded
And the devil will take the rest
All is for the best
Believe in what we're told
Blind men in the market
Buying what we're sold
Believe in what we're told
Until our final breath
While our loving Watchmaker
Loves us all to death

Should something appear unjust to us in this world, the Watchmaker will fix it in the next. All balances will come due.

And the continuity of tracks continues with track three, the title track. Blistering guitar and walls of sound surround the entire listening experience, building in a way Rush has not built since "Jacob's Ladder." Peart carefully avoids too much description of the actual angels. Instead, we the listeners understand what they do to heighten our desires and shelter our curiosity from too much stimulation.

You promise every treasure, to the foolish and the wise
Goddesses of mystery, spirits in disguise
Every pleasure, we bow and close our eyes
Clockwork angels, promise every prize
Clockwork angels, spread their arms and sing
Synchronized and graceful, they move like living things
Goddesses of Light, of Sea and Sky and Land

Much like Pink Floyd's *Animals*, Peart even places the words from actual Proverbs of the Old Testament into the liner notes and lyrics. "Lean not upon your own understanding," Peart's translation of Hebrew reads, while the band shifts to a very blues-based sound. While Peart's universe is not this actual universe, he is clearly tying his story not just to faerie, but to actual Judeo-Christianity. So, while the Watchmaker is not God, and the Anarchist is not the devil, each character most likely sees himself as a powerful representative of the Cosmic struggle.

The fourth track introduces the listener to "The Anarchist," the antagonist of the Watchmaker. Part devil, part terrorist, part bitterness itself, the Anarchist seeks to destabilize all harmony, preferring the very essence of chaos to the essence of any order. Beyond destruction, however, the Anarchist has few goals.

The lenses inside of me that paint the world black
The pools of poison, the scarlet mist, that spill over into rage
The things I've always been denied
An early promise that somehow died
A missing part of me that grows around me like a cage

Whatever his strengths—if any—the Anarchist is and will always remain trapped within the prison of himself. He is an individualist, but to such an extreme that he knows no community. He has abstracted himself from everything and from all.

Having made it to the city, now alienated from all he knew and without the anchor of family and tradition, Hardy stares at the bewildering aspects of the city.

How I prayed just to get away
To carry me anywhere
Sometimes the angels punish us
By answering our prayers

Perhaps he has earned this chaos, he fears. With the story, the protagonist has found a Bradbury-esque like carnival, but the lyrics owe as much to the author of *Something Wicked This Way Comes* as to Jethro Tull's *Aqualung*.

The first five songs have such a tightness of continuity, that the listener has simply found himself fully immersed in the story of this hauntingly familiar universe. With the sixth track, "Halo Effect," the band and the listener finally have time to breathe. A love song of sorts, "Halo Effect" considers the idealistic images we place upon another, especially with infatuation, which we sometimes incorrectly mistake for love.

What did I care?
Fool that I was
Little by little, I burned
Maybe sometimes
There might be a flaw
But how pretty the picture was back then
What did I do?
Fool that I was
To profit from youthful mistakes?
It's shameful to tell
How often I fell
In love with illusions again
So shameful to tell
Just how often I fell
In love with illusions again

The breather over, Rush takes us right back into the world of adventures, "Seven Cities of Gold," and we, along with Hardy, find ourselves following in the footsteps of the greatest explorers of the fifteenth through seventeenth centuries, Conquistadors looking for the lost bishop, Prester John, and his Christian companions.

A man can lose himself, in a country like this
Rewrite the story

Recapture the glory
A man could lose his life, in a country like this
Sunblind and friendless
Frozen and endless

In this land, a man might find himself or simply remake himself anew. The desert, not the ocean, baptizes.

However intense and exciting the adventures, Hardy finds himself alone in "The Wreckers." These folks, perhaps simply wanting to make a life for themselves, have in their own protection, become the unwitting allies of the Anarchist, demolishing in the name of building. Peart uses the story, not unexpectedly, to offer some personal and philosophical reflections.

All I know is that sometimes you have to be wary
Of a miracle too good to be true
All I know is that sometimes the truth is contrary
Everything in life you thought you knew
All I know is that sometimes you have to be wary
'Cause sometimes the target is you

Hardy barely escapes with his life, but he does so at the cost of having seen humanity at its absolute worst.

A rocker of epic proportions, "Headlong Flight" follows Hardy into the unknown, his escape from fire into fire. Leaving the parasitic Wreckers, he encounters even greater dangers. As he does, he reflects on his time, wondering if he should lament his choices, lick his wounds in self-pity, or embrace his scars as badges of honor.

All the highlights of that headlong flight
Holding on with all my might
To what I felt back then
I wish that I could live it all again
I have stoked the fire on the big steel wheels

Steered the airships right across the stars
I learned to fight, I learned to love and learned to feel
Oh, I wish that I could live it all again
All the treasures
The gold and glory
It didn't always feel that way
I don't regret it—
I never forget it—
I wouldn't trade tomorrow for today

Would one live it all again, Peart asks? The song, of course, is as much a retrospective about Peart's real life as it is about Hardy's fictional one.

After a brief return to the tune and themes of fate and free will with "BU2B2," the album concludes with two songs of charity, mercy, and good will. The second to last track, "Wish Them Well," considers all of the people who have betrayed each one of us. Some of them were malicious, while most were probably simply clueless.

The ones who've done you wrong
The ones who pretended to be so strong
The grudges you've held for so long
It's not worth singing that same sad song
Even though you're going through hell
Just keep on going
Let the demons dwell
Just wish them well

In its intent, it is a song of ultimate Stoic virtue.

Playing upon Judeo-Christian theology as well as small-r republican theory—directly referencing the greatest writer of the European Enlightenment, Voltaire—"The Garden" concludes the album on a breathtakingly beautiful note.

The treasure of a life is a measure of love and respect
The way you live, the gifts that you give
In the fullness of time
It's the only return that you expect
The future disappears into memory
With only a moment between
Forever dwells in that moment
Hope is what remains to be seen

Even as the Watchmaker devours our lives in time, events, and his own vision of order, we persist, we live, and we make our own decisions. Just as Stoics have called the slave Epictetus the freest of men and Nero, the Emperor, the most enslaved of men, so Peart calls us to understand that we always have the freedom of soul and of conscience. The evil of others never justifies our own, and in each moment, we can choose to make our own souls commensurate with what is good, true, and beautiful.

Classic Rock magazine gave *Clockwork Angels* a 9 out of 10 and proclaimed it one of the single best albums in the long career of Rush.[27453] Grant Moon of *Prog* could not praise it highly enough.

Marvel at Clockwork Angels *for one or all of its many levels: its literary depth and steampunk cool; its creators' unity of purpose and preternatural musical sense; its lip-curling rock grooves and girthy production. Whatever Raskulinecz is doing, it's working. In the blue sky of this creative Indian summer and with that cultural tailwind behind them, Rush channel the impulse that made them so special all along on a modern progressive album right up there in their canon. After 40 years in a world lit only by lighters, there's no sign they're headed for that garden any time soon.*[54]

Metal Hammer awarded it a 9/10:

Graced with a clear, powerful and imaginative production from Nick Raskulinecz of Foo Fighters, AIC and Velvet Revolver fame, Clockwork Angels *offers a better set of songs than 2007's* Snakes & Arrows *(also helmed by Nick), and is a far more satisfying vehicle for the guitar expertise of Alex Lifeson than 2002's mostly solo-free* Vapor Trails. *It might even be their best and hardest-rocking record since the celebrated* Moving Pictures, *performed in its entirety on their last tour but recorded in 1981. With the keys stripped right back and Alex serving up some down'n'dirty riffing, hearing Rush as a power-trio once again is a beautiful thing.*[55]

A beautiful thing, indeed.

THE END

Rush finished its touring career with its majestic R40 tour, covering much of Canada and the United States. At the end of the tour—at the last show—Neil got down from his drum platform and, much to the surprise of his bandmates, joined them center stage.[56] It was a glorious moment, a glorious end, to a glorious career. The three would never play together again.

With the end of the tour, Peart spent as much time as he could with his family—even serving as a library assistant at his daughter's school—and with his writing. Tragically, in the summer of 2016, something was off with Peart's mental and vocal processes. After some hurried tests, it was discovered that he was suffering from a brain tumor (glioblastoma). Despite an operation in August 2016, his doctors told him that, at best, he had another eighteen months to live. True to Peart's stoic spirit, he fought the cancer with everything he had and lived another three and 1/2 years, finally succumbing on January 7, 2020.[57]

In the final years, when Philip Wilding asked Peart about his life and his career over scotch, he responded: "Remember: nobody's perfect.... So there are no regrets, in the truest sense. And also, I hope someone who likes us, who likes Rush and our music, or admires us as people, can feel that we would never let them down."[58]

1. Peart, *Ghost Rider*, 5.
2. Peart, *Ghost Rider*, 7.
3. Peart, *Ghost Rider*, 8.
4. Peart, *Ghost Rider*, 9.
5. James McNair, "Rock and Pop: Rush's Long Road to Triumph in Rio," *London Independent* (December 12, 2003), 16.
6. Peart, *Ghost Rider*, 10. See also Budofsky, *Modern Drummer Legends: Rush's Neil Peart*, 84.
7. Menon, *Rush: An Oral History Uncensored*.
8. McNair, "Rush's Long Road to Triumph in Rio," 16.
9. Angela Pacienza, "Rejuvenated Rush," *Edmonton Journal* (May 21, 2002), C2.
10. Angela Pacienza, "Rejuvenated Rush," *Edmonton Journal* (May 21, 2002), C2.
11. Alex Lifeson, quoted in David Veitch, "In No Rush: Band Gives Peart Time to Grieve," *Calgary Sun* (October 29, 1998).
12. Peart, *Ghost Rider*, 34.
13. Peart, *Ghost Rider*, 39.
14. Peart, *Ghost Rider*, 310.
15. Peart, *Ghost Rider*, 355
16. Peart, *Ghost Rider*, 146–147.
17. Peart, *Ghost Rider*, 338–339.
18. Paul Elliott, "Everyone Loves Rush," *Classic Rock* (July 2015).
19. Stephen Baldwin, "To His Own Drum," *National Post* (Canada; April 18, 2011), B8; and Peart, *Far and Away*, 200.
20. Peart, "Remembering Andrew," neilpeart.net (January 25, 2012).
21. Steve Stav, "Percussion, Photography Cross Paths in 'Rhythm & Light,'" Ink19.com (July 2005).
22. Peart, *Ghost Rider*, 453–454.
23. Peart, *Ghost Rider*, 455; and Sorelle Saidman, "Ricky Rushes to Release," *Vancouver Province* (September 26, 2000), B4.
24. Peart, *Roadshow*, 81.
25. Carrie Nuttall, "Rhythm and Light: Moments That Otherwise Pass Unnoticed," introduction to her *Rhythm & Light* (Cambridge, MA: Rounder, 2005). No page numbers are employed in the book.
26. Nuttall, "Rhythm and Light."
27. Scott Iwasaki, "Photos Dramatize 'Rhythm and Light,'" *Deseret News* (June 17, 2005).
28. Peart, "My Rhythm, Her Light," in Nuttall, *Rhythm & Light*.
29. Peart, *Far and Near*, 303. See also Lee and Lifeson's comments in Paul Elliott, "Everybody Loves Rush," *Classic Rock* (July 2015).
30. McNair, "Rush's Long Road to Triumph in Rio," 16.
31. Menon, *Rush: An Oral History Uncensored*.
32. Steve Morse, "Vapor Trails Follow 6-Year Hiatus," *Hamilton Spectator* (May 13, 2002), C8.
33. Angela Pacienza, "Rejuvenated Rush," *Edmonton Journal* (May 21, 2002), C2.
34. Steve Morse, "Vapor Trails Follow 6-Year Hiatus," *Hamilton Spectator* (May 13, 2002), C8.
35. Menon, *Rush: An Oral History Uncensored*.

36. Sandra Sperounes, "Rush: Arena Rockers Hit Concert Trail," *Edmonton Journal* (September 8, 2002), B1.
37. Eric R. Danton, "Rush: A Relic Refreshed," *Hartford Courant* (Jun 28, 2002).
38. Philip Wilding, "The Classic Rock Interview: Geddy Lee," *Classic Rock* (December 2018), 44.
39. Sandra Sperounes, "Rush: Arena Rockers Hit Concert Trail," *Edmonton Journal* (September 8, 2002), B1.
40. Peart "said he meant it in the song to symbolize the afterimage or afterglow of Selena and Jackie, a distant ephemeral version of the original." Kevin J. Anderson to author, personal note, April 30, 2021.
41. "Peart Reveals Literary Inspirations Behind Rush Album," *Jam! Showbiz* (May 31, 2002).
42. Richard Abowitz, *Rolling Stone* (April 24, 2002).
43. Mac Randall, "*Vapor Trails* Review," *Guitar World* (June 2002).
44. Andrew Tuttle, "*Vapor Trails* Review," *Orange County Register* (May 20, 2002).
45. Christa L. Titus, "Spotlight Review: Vapor Trails," *Billboard* (May 18, 2002).
46. Menon, *Rush: An Oral History Uncensored*.
47. Peart, *Far and Away*, 116.
48. Menon, *Rush: An Oral History Uncensored*.
49. Menon, *Rush: An Oral History Uncensored*.
50. Rob Sheffield, *Snakes and Arrows* Album Review, *Rolling Stone* (May 14, 2007).
51. Geoff Barton, "Snakes Alive!" *Classic Rock* (June 2007).
52. Lee quoted in Paul Elliott, "Everyone Loves Rush," *Classic Rock* (July 2015), 41.
53. Dave Everley, "Rush's 20th Release is Their First Concept Album. It's Also One of the Best Albums of their Career," *Classic Rock* (July 2012).
54. Grant Moon, "*Clockwork Angels* Review," *Prog* (July 2012).
55. Dave Ling, "Seminal Prog Rockers Hit a High Note," *Metal Hammer* (July 2012).
56. Peart, *Far and Wide: Bring that Horizon to Me!* (ECW, 2016), 278–279.
57. Brian Hiatt tells the story of Peart's last few years brilliantly in his "The Spirit of Neil Peart," *Rolling Stone* (January 7, 2021). *Rolling Stone*, all is forgiven! It should be noted, the article is a "digital exclusive."
58. Philip Wilding, "Neil Peart, September 12, 1952–January 7, 2020," *Classic Rock* (March 2020): 15. Wilding's final articles about Peart in *Prog* and *Classic Rock* are nothing short of breathtaking and stunning in their emotion as well as in their appreciation.

CONCLUSION

Despite having legions of fans, the three members of Rush all remained perplexed at their continued success and the undying praise awarded by their fans. When fans appeared at the airport in Brazil to greet the band in 2002, Geddy expressed shock. "Listen, we're musicians. It's not really that noble of a pursuit. If we can do something that touches someone like that, it's really mind-boggling to me."[1] When the producers and writers of the major movie documentary, *Beyond the Lighted Stage*, first approached Rush, they responded with hesitation.

"We kinda know how boring we are, or just sort of ordinary, and we weren't sure that they'd have anything that would be particularly exciting," Lifeson explains. *"But they stayed on us and eventually won us over. And they did a great job with it. It tells an interesting story that a lot of people can relate to, and at the same time it's kind of unique and different."*[2]

As every Rush fan knows, however, part of their middle-class ordinary-ness is what makes them so appealing. They could be us. That is, if we worked that hard and had that many smarts!

Whatever sincere shock they express regarding their achievements and their fan recognition of the same, Peart, Lifeson, and Lee are fascinating. Other prominent twentieth-century artists, such as T.S. Eliot and J.R.R. Tolkien, led middle-class lives as well. Frankly, this makes them more interesting, not less. They led lives like many others of intelligence, good will, and purpose, but they do so with something extra as well. It's *that something else* that matters so much. They have successfully avoided the pitfalls and immoralities that often accompany fame, certainly common in the rock world; they have paved their own way to success; they have never quit, whatever the opposition (internal or external); and they obviously love excellence, what they do, and each other.

Yet it is admittedly difficult to gauge exactly how influential Rush and Peart have been. One can readily count the numbers of books Peart has sold—with or without Kevin J. Anderson. One can also readily identify just how many albums, DVDs, etc., Rush has sold. But to what effect? When J.R.R. Tolkien sells millions and millions of copies of *The Lord of the Rings*, no one questions his significance. Many—especially an older generation of literary critics—may very well dislike the fact of Tolkien's success, but no sane person denies his popularity and his influence on countless women and men. The band had sold over forty million albums by 2004, their thirtieth anniversary, with the RIAA certifying twenty-four as gold, fourteen as platinum, and three as multiplatinum. Not too bad for three nice young men from eastern Canada. Yet, what does it mean? If we examine Tolkien, we can find the themes of *The Lord of the Rings* throughout our current culture. But, what about Rush? It's not unusual for a fan of *The Lord of the Rings* to read the trilogy every so many years, probably accounting for a total of ten to fifteen reads per lifetime. What about Rush? If Rush sold forty million albums by 2004, how do we register the influence? What Rush fan has only listened to "Tom Sawyer" a mere fifteen times, equivalent to reading Tolkien's trilogy, at least in terms of quantifying? The average Rush fan might very well have heard "Tom Sawyer" several hundred times (or more) in his lifetime: on the radio, in concert, through numerous plays of *Moving Pictures* and various live concert albums and videos, on television shows, even in the supermarket. How could Peart's words from the song not become a significant part of a listener's life?

Of all periodicals, strangely, the one that spent so much of its own existence mocking the band, *Rolling Stone* finally got it right in 2012:

Over the decades, Rush learned to accept and even embrace their reputation as the ultimate dorky band. "Not only were we vilified, but our fans were too," says Peart. "In the schoolyard you'd hear, 'Oh, what do you know? You're a Rush fan.'" But the band has made an unexpected leap into mainstream pop culture in the past four years—including a much-buzzed-about 2008 appearance on The Colbert Report *and a genuinely hilarious cameo in 2009s Paul Rudd–Jason Siegel comedy* I Love You, Man. *The PR boost has helped Rush sell out venues around the US. "It feels like vindication," Peart says. "We set a good example by showing people you can do things your way and still succeed."*[3]

Longtime fan and accomplished author Robert Freedman, however, got it even more correct than did *Rolling Stone*.

The story of Rush is a story of validation. When the band first started out, the mainstream music establishment largely ignored them. Geddy's voice was the brunt of jokes, Alex's guitar playing got no respect, Neil's lyrics were pretentious and channeled a kooky Ayn Randian ideology, and he played too many drums, all of them with the passion of a mathematician. Meanwhile, musicians and music aficionados loved them, so you had this great narrative tension. Now they're nearing their 40-year anniversary, their old critics are in nursing homes, their fans are in leadership positions in business, science, government, and the arts, and they're looked to as elder statesmen of rock.[4]

If a person knows almost nothing else about Peart, he almost certainly knows of him as one of the best drummers in rock history. Justly, this reputation adheres to Peart and almost certainly will continue to do so for a very long time. Two journalists for the *Vancouver Sun* stated it well in 2011. "Who's Neil Peart?" asks one. The other answers: "Well, the shared consensus of fans and industry personnel alike is that Neil Peart is possibly the greatest talent to ever sit behind a drum kit."[5] This was not the first time such a thing was written, and it will almost certainly not be the last.

Perhaps the *A.V. Club* got it right, too, when the venerable website labeled Rush "The Biggest Cult Band in the World."[6] They had not been the first do so, and they will certainly not be the last. *Mojo* proclaimed Rush's success as the "revenge of the nerds."[7] While the majority of reviewers have appreciated Rush over their forty-some year history, a small but very powerful and vocal minority besmirched the band whenever and wherever possible. For now, it's worth noting that when it came to the mainstream media, Rush remained the ultimate underdogs until very recently. The most elite of the elite newspapers, *The New York Times*, provides a perfect glimpse into how the mainstream looks at Rush. In 1979, the venerable paper's reviewer reported, after watching the trio play at the Palladium, "the whole thing seems busy and empty in the manner of too many of these souped-up, neo-King Crimson outfits."[8] Fifteen years later, the paper claimed a Rush concert "not so much a collection of songs as a nonstop technological force," with the band bringing order to the chaos of the lives of its teenage audience, "like a sonic video game."[9] Three years later, in 1994, the newspaper claimed that Rush possessed no ability to vary its dynamics. "Like the walls of a musical fortress, the band's unyielding performance keeps insiders protected and outsiders away," it believed.[10] Clearly, the most elite of all American newspapers felt more than a bit jilted and a bit left out. Almost twenty years after the first review, the band seemed nearly the same, the then-arts writers for the *Times* proclaimed. "The presentation was so hard and shiny that it was nearly impossible to discern whether the players were having a good or bad night," it wrote.[11] By 2007, however, the *Times* grudgingly acknowledged the longevity and energy of the band, offering a mostly factual review of their Madison Square Garden concert for *Snakes and Arrows*. "The trio plays with unrelenting muscle, pounding out the intricacies of its songs, but rarely letting them breathe," it noted in unusually restrained fashion.[12] In 2010, the paper decided simply to label Rush "that long-running and consistently bizarre Canadian hard-rock band" but found Peart the most interesting member, even if "reclusive and ornery."[13]

Looking back over Rush's career in 1988, Peart remembered how painful the criticism could be, but also how the band went their own way:

"There have always been these factions in rock 'n' roll that absolutely hated us—we're used to that," he said. "But we've always been happy with the way we achieved success. It didn't come from a lot of good press and exposure, or because we were critics' darlings. It was a result of the real thing—because we got out there and slogged around the US. We were a hardworking touring group and we stayed on the road as much as we could. We choose that avenue—we believed that it was the natural order of things, and it worked for us."[14]

Peart, however, is much more than "merely" a drummer and a lyricist for a power trio.

SOME FINAL WORDS

I began this book with the following from Kevin J. Anderson and Peart from *Clockwork Lives*: "Some lives can be summed up in a sentence or two. Other lives are epics."[15] These words are as true now as they were 55,000 words ago. No rational person could sum up Peart's life in a sentence or two, meaning that phrases such as "world's greatest drummer" or "best rock lyricist" or "one of our finest men of letters" simply do not do justice to the complexity, the life, the mind, and the perseverance of Neil Ellwood Peart.

Throughout this book, I have done my best to prove the latter two claims, finest lyricist and man of letters. From my very uneducated perspective, he is also the world's best drummer. Many fellow males of the Western Hemisphere would certainly agree with me.

I have also done my best to show that—whatever the professional critics might think—the sale of Rush albums, the success of Peart's books (critically as well as financially), and the direct statements of musicians provide ample evidence to demonstrate just how influential Peart is.

But for most of us who admire Peart, we cannot directly show just how his words or his character or his music or his personality have affected us on a day-by-day basis.

As I mentioned at the beginning of this work, I first encountered the music of Rush in 1981, when I was just thirteen. At that time, my family life was not just dysfunctional, it was violent, chaotic, and suffocating. Like any teenager, I was struggling to find who I was, but I did so in a domestic jungle. But I also had to figure out how to survive. And please believe me, survival was not a sure thing. Home was hell. But, *Moving Pictures* and *Signals* gave me great strength, and *Grace Under Pressure* even more so.

Peart stated repeatedly that he did not always appreciate his fans and their rabidity, especially the fanatics and those who read secret messages in his lyrics. I never read anything into his lyrics except this: be yourself, find your gifts, hone your gifts, and always wield integrity. And all of this should be done, no matter the cost. I never once felt that Peart wanted to make a world of little Pearts, each conformed to his image. Rather, as all true individualists, he wanted to leaven everything through his own excellence and remind us of the most important things in life.

I'm an Individualist. I believe in the greatness of individual people. That's not anti-populist or anti-human. When the lights come on behind us, and I look out at the audience and see all those little circles, each of those circles is a person. Each person is a story. They have circumstances surrounding their lives that can never be repeated.... I'm always playing for an individual. I don't play for the crowd — for some faceless ideal of commerciality of some lowest common denominator. It's a person up there every night, who knows everything I'm supposed to do. If I don't do it, that person knows it. It's like I have a judge on my shoulder, in the old Anglo-Saxon way, who watches everything I play. If I play it right, my judge says, 'Not bad.' And if I play it wrong, it's 'You jerk.' That individual is the person I play for every night.[16]

And this he did. Throughout my life, Peart's words have reminded me of the most important things. Whether he wrote these words in lyrics, in his books, or spoke them in interviews.

Peart made me more myself, not less.

And while I cannot prove it, I'm pretty sure I speak for thousands upon thousands of others who have been inspired by Neil Peart's spirit beyond the gilded stage.

---

1. Geddy Lee, "The Boys in Brazil," a documentary by Andrew Macnaughton.
2. Gary Graff, "Rush: The Next Stage," *Classic Rock* (August 2010).
3. Andy Greene, "Inside Rush's New Sci-Fi Rock Opera," *Rolling Stone* (June 5, 2012).
4. Robert Freedman, "Why *Clockwork Angels* Will Be Made into a Movie," *Rush Vault* (online resource, June 29, 2012). This is not to suggest that all of those who have mocked Peart's lyrics have suddenly repented and seen the light. Reuters reported in 2007 that Peart came in second as the worst lyricist of all times, bested (worsted?) only by Gordan Sumner (Sting). See "Sting Tops List of Worst Lyricists," *Reuters* of Los Angeles (October 9, 2007).
5. Marissa Baecker and Jasmin Doobay, "The Sound When Music and Motorcycles Collide," *Vancouver Sun* (November 4, 2011), G13.
6. Jason Heller, "Gateway to Geekery," *A.V. Club* (August 1, 2013); and Ian Harvey, Birmingham (ENG) *Express and Star* (March 8, 2011).

7. Paul Elliott, "Revenge of the Nerds," *Mojo* (June 2012).
8. John Rockwell, "Pop: Rush Plays at Palladium," *New York Times* (January 15, 1979), C17.
9. Karen Schoemer, "More Technological than Human," *New York Times* (December 11, 1991), C22.
10. Jon Pareles, "A 20-Year-Old Band with Some New Tricks," *New York Times* (March 10, 1994), C16.
11. Ben Ratliff, "Years Later, Still Mad at the World," *New York Times* (December 18, 1996), C20.
12. Jon Pareles, "Arena Rock with a Worldview and all the Flash Trimmings," *New York Times* (September 19, 2007), E5.
13. Jon Caramanica, "Wizards When They Play, Certainly," *New York Times* (June 26, 2010), C6.
14. Peart quoted in Bob Claypool, "Interview with Neil Peart," *Houston Post* (January 27, 1988).
15. Kevin J. Anderson and Neil Peart, *Clockwork Lives* (ECW, 2015), frontispiece.
16. Budofsky, *Modern Drummer Legends: Rush's Neil Peart*, 24.

BIBLIOGRAPHY

Studio Albums with Rush

Fly by Night (Mercury 1975)
Caress of Steel (Mercury 1975)
2112 (Mercury 1976)
A Farewell to Kings (Mercury 1977)
Hemispheres (Mercury 1978)
Permanent Waves (Mercury 1980)
Moving Pictures (Mercury 1981)
Signals (Mercury 1982)
Grace Under Pressure (Mercury 1983)
Power Windows (Mercury 1985)
Hold Your Fire (Mercury 1987)
Presto (Atlantic 1989)
Roll the Bones (Atlantic 1991)
Counterparts (Atlantic 1993)
Test for Echo (Atlantic 1996)
Vapor Trails (Atlantic 2002); *Vapor Trails Remixed* (Atlantic 2013)
Feedback (Atlantic 2004)
Snakes and Arrows (Atlantic 2007)
Clockwork Angels (Roadrunner 2012)

Live Albums with Rush

ABC 1974 (Leftfield 2011)
All the World's a Stage (Mercury 1976)
Exit ... Stage Left (Mercury 1981)
Grace Under Pressure Tour (Mercury 1984)
A Show of Hands (Mercury 1989)
Different Stages (Atlantic 1998)
Rush in Rio (Atlantic 2003)
R30 (Atlantic 2005)
Snakes and Arrows Live (Atlantic 2008)
Working Men (Atlantic 2009)
Time Machine Tour (Roadrunner 2011)
Clockwork Angels Tour (Roadrunner 2013)
R40 (Anthem 2014)

Other Musical Works by Peart

Burning for Buddy (Atlantic 1994)
Anatomy of a Drum Solo (Hudson 2005)
Neil Peart: A Work in Progress (Alfred 2002, 2006)
The Making of Burning for Buddy (Alfred 2006)
Rush, 2112/Moving Pictures: Classic Albums (Eagle 2010)
Fire on Ice (Drumchannel.com 2010)
Taking Center Stage: A Lifetime of Live Performance (Hudson 2011)

With Other Bands

Vertical Horizon, *Burning the Days* (Outfall 2009)
Sonic Elements, *XYZ: A Tribute to Rush* (Sonic Reality 2012)
Vertical Horizon, *Echoes from the Underground* (Outfall 2013)

Books/Stories by Peart

"*Drumbeats*" by Kevin J. Anderson and Neil Peart (1994; Word-

Fire Press 2011, 2020)

Masked Rider: Cycling in West Africa (1996; ECW 2004)

Ghost Writer: Travels on the Healing Road (ECW 2002)

Traveling Music: The Soundtrack to My Life and Times (ECW 2004)

Roadshow Landscape with Drums: A Concert Tour by Motorcycle (Rounder 2006)

"Introduction" to *Landscapes* by Kevin J. Anderson (Five Star 2006)

Far and Away: A Prize Every Time (ECW 2011)

Clockwork Angels, by Kevin J. Anderson based on a story and lyrics by Neil Peart (ECW 2012)

Clockwork Angels, six-part comic series, by Kevin J. Anderson, Neil Peart, and Nick Robles (BOOM! Studios 2013/2014)

Far and Near: On Days Like These (ECW 2014)

Clockwork Lives, by Kevin J. Anderson and Neil Peart (ECW 2015)

Far and Wide: Bring That Horizon to Me! (ECW 2016)

Clockwork Lives: The Graphic Novel, by Kevin J. Anderson and Neil Peart (Insight 2018)

Rush Backstage Club Newsletters, 1980–1994 (ShowTech 2020).

Clockwork Destiny, by Kevin J. Anderson and Neil Peart
ECW Press, June 2022.

Works Relevant to Rush or Progressive Rock

Kevin J. Anderson, *Clockwork Angels: The Comic Scripts* (WordFire Press 2014)

Roie Avin, *Essential Modern Progressive Rock Albums: Images and Words Behind Prog's Most Celebrated Albums, 1990–2016* (Royal Avenue Media 2017)

Bill Banasiewicz, *Rush Visions: The Official Biography* (Omnibus 1988)

Joe Bergamini, *Taking Center Stage: A Lifetime of Live Performance, Neil Peart* (Hudson 2012)

Durrell Bowman, *Experiencing Rush: A Listener's Companion* (Rowman and Littlefield 2015)

Jim Berti and Durrell Bowman, eds., *Rush and Philosophy: Heart and Mind United* (Open Court 2011).

Bill Bruford, *The Autobiography* (Jawbone 2009)

Adam Budofsky, ed., *Modern Drummer Legends: Rush's Neil Peart* (2020).

Classic Rock Presents Rush: Clockwork Angels (2012)

Jon Collins, *Rush: Chemistry* (Helter Skelter 2005)

Skip Daley and Eric Hansen, *Rush: Wandering the Face of the Earth: The Official Touring History, 1968–2015* (Insight 2019)

Jerry Ewing, ed., *Prog: Rush, Limited Edition* (Prog, issue 35, April 2013)

Jerry Ewing, *Wonderous Stories: A Journey Through the Landscape of Progressive Rock* (Flood Gallery 2017)

Peter Erskine, *No Beethoven: An Autobiography and Chronicle of Weather Report* (Fuzz/E/Books 2013)

Robert Freedman, *Rush: Life, Liberty, and the Pursuit of Excellence* (Algora 2014)

Steve Hogarth, *The Invisible Man Diaries, 1991–1997* (Miwk 2014)

Steve Hogarth, *The Invisible Man Diaries, 1998–2014* (Miwk 2014)

Stephen Humphries, *Art of Rush: Hugh Syme, Serving a Life Sentence* (2112 Books, 2015)

Stephen Lambe, *Citizens of Hope and Glory: The Story of Progressive Rock* (2011; Amberley 2014)

Geddy Lee, *Geddy Lee's Big Beautiful Book of Bass: A Compendium of the Rare, Iconic, and Weird* (HarperCollins 2018)

Edward Macan, *Rocking the Classics: English Progressive Rock and the Counterculture* (Oxford 1997)

Chris McDonald, *Rush: Rock Music and the Middle Class, Dreaming in Middletown* (Bloomington: Indiana University Press 2009)

Lori Majewski and Jonathan Bernstein, *Mad World: An Oral History of New Wave Artists and Songs that Defined the 1980s* (New York: Abrams Image 2014)

Vinay Menon, *Rush: An Oral History Uncensored* (Star Dispatches 2013)

BIBLIOGRAPHY

Max Mobley, *Rush FAQ: All That Left to Know about Rock's Greatest Power Trio* (Backbeat 2014)

Carrie Nuttall, *Rhythm and Light* (Rounder 2005)

Martin Popoff, *Anthem: Rush in the '70s* (ECW 2020)

Martin Popoff, *Contents Under Pressure: 30 Years of Rush at Home and Away* (ECW 2004)

Martin Popoff, *Limelight: Rush in the '80s* (ECW 2020)

Martin Popoff, *Rush: Album by Album* (Quarton 2017)

Martin Popoff, *Rush: The Illustrated History* (Voyageur Press 2013)

Carol Selby Price and Robert M. Price, *Mystic Rhythms: The Philosophical Vision of Rush* (Gillette, NJ 1999)

Will Romano, *Mountains Come Out of the Sky: The Illustrated History of Prog Rock* (Backbeat 2010)

Will Romano, *Prog Rock FAQ: All That's Left to Know about Rock's Most Progressive Music* (Backbeat 2014)

Robert Telleria, *Rush Tribute: Merely Players* (Kingston, ONT: Quarry Music Books 2002)

Jeff Wagner, *Mean Deviation: Four Decades of Progressive Heavy Metal* (Bazillion Points 2010)

Rich Wilson, *Lifting Shadows: The Authorized Biography of Dream Theater* (Rocket 88 2013)

Best Websites

2112.net/powerwindows
rush.com
rushisaband.com
rushtheband.com
rushvault.com

Personal Correspondence and Conversations

With Kevin J. Anderson, Robin Armstrong, Steve Babb, Mike Barnett, Pete Blum, Craig Breaden, Andrew Craske, John Deasey, Dom DiGiovanni, Carl Olson, Jeff Deist, Allison Henderson, Erik Heter, Steve Horwitz (RIP), Stephen Humphries, Geddy Lee Israel, James Joseph, Kevin McCormick, John J. Miller, Rebecca Moesta, Chris Morrissey, Ivan Pongracic, Aeon Skoble, Sarah Skwire, Greg Spawton, Matt Stevens, Roine Stolt, Andy Tillison, Tad Wert, and Kevin Williams.

APPENDIX A
WHAT IS PROGRESSIVE ROCK?

Though rooted deeply in the rock tradition, especially in its more innovative aspects as explored in the 1960s, Rush is usually identified as practitioners of progressive rock. Their progressive rock, however, is not an imitation of Yes or Genesis, but a building upon it and a branching out from it, continuously. In Rush's style of progressive, heavy metal, jazz, ska, reggae, grunge, and a myriad of styles fuse into one.

It is not unusual for those outside of the prog world, especially in North America, to ask in confusion "Progressive rock?" "What is that? It sounds as if Woodrow Wilson, Teddy Roosevelt, Margaret Sanger, and John Dewey have formed a band. Nothing progressive is good."

The fact is, progressive rock is nearly indefinable. Even those credited with making progressive rock reject the title as often as not. Prog fans, too, obsess over what group or album or (less likely) song is or is not progressive. Once there's some semblance of an agreement as to prog quality, the fans then obsess over what type of progressive rock the group or album in question is: symphonic; proto-; crossover; metal; post-; folk; math; space; fusion; Kraut; Canterbury.

Several things can be stated definitively (well, somewhat) regarding what progressive rock entails.

First, it's almost always full of really odd and variable time signatures, sometimes within just a few moments of a song. Rarely does the common rock/pop/jazz signature of 4/4 predominate. It happens, but often as a brief moment between 7/8 and 9/8. Much of this is inspired by late 1950s jazz, such as that by the Dave Brubeck Quartet and by a number of impressionist jazz groups. Rush famously writes music with constantly changing time signatures, but they do it so well that few non-musicians notice it.

Second, while in its specifics prog is fully open to music from all times and all places, the world over, progressive rock generally is very European in its structure and in the atmosphere it creates. Because progressive rock has always tended to sidestep or ignore blues-based rock, mainstream and elitist periodicals such as *Rolling Stone* and the *New Music Express* and journals of opinion such as the *New York Times* have assumed progressive rock is a betrayal of progressive culture rather than an embracing or enhancing of it. After a very short flirtation with prog, music critics rejected the genre as pretentious and over-the-top.

Though "progressive jazz" had been used as a term of approbation for non-trendy, non-danceable jazz since the 1920s, the term "progressive rock" saw print for the first time in the English language only in 1968, in the *Chicago Tribune*. The mention carried no deep disgust or praise, just a recognition that this was not regular pop or rock. In the summer of the same year, the *New York Times* lamented that by making "the leap from sewer to salon, pop music has ceased to be an adventure." Though "musically advanced," progressive rock had made its art "emotionally barren." Even the most intellectual of critics, the paper continued, could see that the "new, cerebral audience has endangered that raw vitality" of rock. A few months later, the *Times* again proclaimed that the "rock hero (who is almost always a social outcast) is a liberator in musician's drag. His sexual display in the face of institutionalized repression becomes an act of rebellion."

Third, prog is rarely about attitude, unlike much rock music (think everyone from Elvis to the Rolling Stones to the Ramones), or about fame (think everyone from the early Beatles to Madonna to Lady Gaga), or about social change (think everyone from Buffalo Springfield to Janis Joplin to Bono), but about serious, penetrating, and pervasive art. As art, prog certainly can include attitude, fame, social change, and almost anything else imaginable, but none of these things serves as the prime motivator in progressive rock. Art does. Nothing could be more true for Rush, who will do almost anything to preserve the integrity of their art.

Fourth, as mentioned in the second point, progressive artists thoroughly enjoy creating an atmosphere, sometimes a self-contained world through which the entire package is birthed: the music, the lyrics, the album art, as well as the live presentation. As to live performances, no group or person took this further than Peter Gabriel did when he served as lead singer and flautist for Genesis in the first half of the 1970s. Gabriel would don a myriad of costumes and act out a variety of roles, often spontaneously and to the surprise of the other members of the group. The outrageous costumes hindered not only the projection of Gabriel's voice, but, through his clumsiness, the integrity of the equipment necessary for live performance.

In regards to album art, one can almost always identify a Talk Talk album by its James Marsh cover, a Big Big Train album by its Jim Trainer cover, and a Rush album by its Hugh Syme cover. But of the artists associated with prog acts, Roger Dean is probably the most famous and iconic. His art for the English group, Yes—found on the front and back covers as well as in the inside sleeves and liner notes—in the early 1970s is not only gorgeous but inviting. The themes evolved gradually from album to album. Often, Dean's art depicted lush worlds, held together in a mystical fashion, with technology serving people in a humane and organic way. While there was a hippie-ish element in the scenes, they were no more outrageous than what Romano Guardini promoted in the 1920s, Wilhelm Röpke and Russell Kirk in the 1950s, and Robert Heinlein in the 1960s.

Perhaps the most important aspect of progressive rock is found in this fourth point. Progressive rock does not aim to move the heart or the passions in the way most rock music does. Instead, it aims to harmonize soul and mind and connect the horizontal to the vertical, the sea to the sky. It invites the listener in as a participant, immersing him fully into the art rather than placing the art (if most pop music can be called art) next to or near the listener. As such, progressive rock is to rock music what Imagism (e.g., T.E. Hulme and T.S. Eliot) is to poetry. It takes a modern form, and it fills and animates it with a well-ordered soul, an essence commensurate with its form. Not surprisingly, Neil Peart greatly admired Eliot, and many of his lyrics, as noted throughout this book, could rightly be regarded as Imagist.

But again, prog rock is not easily defined. A fifth and final point about its definition is this: Progressive rock concepts rarely can be explained in the span of a two- or three-minute song. Genesis took 94 minutes to tell the story of Rael in "The Lamb Lies Down"; Rush took 21 minutes to tell the story of failure to resist tyranny in "2112"; Jethro Tull needed 44 minutes for the story of Gerald Bostock in "Thick as a Brick"; Marillion took 71 minutes to reveal a suicide in "Brave"; and Big Big Train took 58 minutes for a man to die and examine his life in "The Difference Machine."

Unlike any other form of popular music, progressive rock always takes its time in developing, and it often plays with notions of time, not just in the time signatures, but in the lyrics and the concepts as well. While J.R.R. Tolkien probably never listened to progressive rock (though Arthur C. Clarke did), it's hard to believe his elves in Rivendell or Lothlorien did not. Even jazz has only a few examples of concept albums, such as Miles Davis's brilliant *Sketches of Spain*. In this, progressive rock has far more in common with ancient and medieval poetic epics, eighteenth century symphonies, and nineteenth century song cycles and opera than it does with current forms of popular art and music.

Rush, in particular, both defies and defines progressive rock. In its first album, without Neil Peart, it embraced a sort of Zeppelin-esque hard or acid rock, with party elements thrown in. *Fly by Night* serves as a transitional album, while *Caress of Steel*, *2112*, *A Farewell to Kings*, *Hemispheres*, and *Clockwork Angels* reveal Rush's epic prog side. One might label *Permanent Waves*, *Moving Pictures*, *Signals*, *Grace Under Pressure*, and *Power Windows* as new wave prog, with *Hold Your Fire* as a jazz-fusion album. *Presto*, *Roll the Bones*, and *Counterparts* all embrace pop-rock-grunge elements, while *Test for Echo*, *Vapor Trails*, and *Snakes and Arrows* offer a very new style of prog rock, driven with strong blues elements and as well as classical tropes.

Yet, even after 55,000 words, I can state with some certainty: Rush is indefinable.

It is what it is.

APPENDIX B
MY LETTER TO NEIL PEART, 2008

Mr. Neil Peart

SRO Management Inc./Anthem Entertainment Group
189 Carlton St
Toronto, ON M5A 2K7
CANADA

August 14, 2008

Dear Mr. Peart,

This is just a short letter to say thank you for your meaningful book, *Ghost Rider: Travels on the Healing Road*. While I found the entire thing riveting from beginning to end, I was especially touched by pages 198–199 and 310–311 regarding your experiences in Catholic churches; page 325 regarding people coming into life when you most need them; page 355 on the basic nature of art; and page 359—"what I am supposed to tell *those* guys?"

In terms of writing style, *Ghost Rider* struck me forcefully as a cross between Jack Kerouac's and Willa Cather's various works (especially Cather's *The Professor's House*), with a number of wonderful "Peartisms" sprinkled throughout.

For what it's worth, I'm terribly sorry for your losses. A year ago today, my wife and I buried one of our children, Cecilia Rose. I started your book a week ago, and it helped me—in ways I could never describe in words—get through this past week. Like you, I wonder about "that other guy," the one who lived before the death of a daughter, and I wonder about the future. Amazingly, this past year coincided with an academic sabbatical, and, in addition to time spent with my family, I also traveled extensively, researched, and completed my next book. Again, *Ghost Rider* offered me great insights into suffering and recovery, and I thank you for it.

I'm enclosing an intellectual biography of J.R.R. Tolkien I published a few years ago. I very much hope you enjoy it, and I hope it, in some way, repays you for the many insights and inspirations your words have offered me over the past twenty-seven years.

Yours,

[It should be noted, Peart responded by sending me a signed postcard—which now safely resides, framed, on my office wall.]

APPENDIX C
INFLUENCE ON MUSICIANS

Peart has inspired innumerable musicians. When Peart died, *Modern Drummer* made a call for appraisals and appreciations. As the editor of *Modern Drummer*, Adam Budofsky wrote, the submissions were somewhat stunning. "In fact, some of the most astute observations and heartfelt remembrances came from the indie, country, world-music, and jazz drummers we contacted," he explained. "For so many of them, Neil was their entry point into drumming, their first and therefore most important musical role model."[1]

In America, no person benefited more from the inspiration of Neil Peart than did Mike Portnoy, a generation younger than Peart, and known for his astounding drumming in progressive and metal bands. "I can't possibly overstate how much influence Rush had on me as a young teenager," the former drummer for Dream Theater said in April 2015. "I would say from about 1981 to 1987, they were my gods. Neil Peart was my god at that point.... The size of the drum set, the way I approached the drums, the odd time signatures, the progressive-styled instrumental music—I mean, just everything about Rush at that point, when I was a developing teenager, was huge." Portnoy has seen them on every tour since the early 1980s.[2] Thirteen years earlier, he had stated something quite similar.

Rush's impact on mine and Dream Theater's lives and career is immeasurable. I think it is pretty safe to say that if it weren't for Rush, there would be no Dream Theater! When I met John Petrucci and John Myung at the Berklee College of Music in the Fall of 1985, there were two immediate things we found we had in common: 1) our home base of Long Island, NY and, 2) our love (no ... make that OBSESSION) with Rush.[3]

Portnoy, it should be noted, is as spirited as they come, and he wears his influences rather openly in good American, New York fashion.

It's worth looking across the ocean to someone a bit more reserved to get his take as well. One prominent English progressive musician, composer Robin Armstrong of Cosmograf, explains in loving detail just how influential the Canadian is:

Neil Peart is one of those drummers that define the band they play for. Bonham was the same for Zeppelin, you can't help but feel certain that the sound of the bands they were in, was built around their technique and unique approach. Peart made technical drumming and its study, very cool in an era when it was really all about gut feel. He inspired many to pick up the sticks and learn the intricate art in drumming. Playing simple songs would never be enough to show off his talent and it's only when you study some of his drum solo performances that you fully get the measure of the precision of his craft. Precise rudiments and super complex poly rhythms leading some of his critics to label him a human drum machine. Such comment is to denigrate his prestigious technique. It sounds perfect because of the sheer ability of the playing. One of the many interesting things he did was seek to reinvent his own style and push it into a more jazz oriented technique later in his career. Humbly accepting the tutelage of those who many would consider lesser players, he has furthered his own amazing repertoire. Surely this is the mark of an amazing artist. Add to this, his contributions as the main lyric writer for Rush and it's difficult not to be convinced that he is the sound of the band.[4]

Certainly, no faint praise, especially from an Englishman. Matt Stevens of The Fierce and the Dead, arguably the most innovative and up-and-coming guitarist on the music scene today, claims that it was Rush's daring that inspired him, rather than Peart's words.

Being from the UK and hanging around the metal/punk/prog/indie scene I never really came across Ayn Rand until a couple of years ago, so it didn't really make any difference to my love of the band, I didn't pay much attention. I know that's wrong, but it's true. I don't share their views but I like that they are trying to make interesting statements. Peart is a clever dude.[5]

Another English musician, referenced earlier in the book, Andy Tillison, lead singer and touchstone of the critically acclaimed band The Tangent, presents Peart in similar terms and with equal enthusiasm.

The idea of a drumming lyricist who brought Coleridge and Nietzsche to the air punching leather-clad audiences of stadia around the world is one that impresses me every time I think of the band and their work. Whatever it was that the negative journalism of the era found so pretentious about Rush and their kind was embraced by Peart and pushed forward. The positivity of the man's work is a force unto itself. I am glad I lived in the world he did.[6]

Tillison speaks for all of us who love Peart. We're glad to live in the world at the same time he did.

American prog rock bassist and lyricist, Steve Babb, of Glass Hammer, offers equally effusive praise of Rush and of Peart.

It sounds silly to say that a particular rock group changed the course of my life, but that's what happened with Rush. I was sixteen when I discovered Fly by Night *and bought it—only because of the name of one song,* Rivendell. *I was already a huge fan of Tolkien (another who altered the course of my life and improved it greatly). I fell in love with their sound and started buying up their albums. The second concert I ever attended was the* Farewell to Kings *show in my hometown. So, about the course alteration, after watching them play I knew I wanted to be a bassist / keyboardist of my own band. I achieved* this by 1980 with Wizards, a popular metal band in Chattanooga that later toured the East Coast. There was no going back. I even had the Taurus Pedals and the synth rig! Watching Geddy Lee made me want to be a great bassist, and I spent hours and hours learning their songs and practicing to their records. From reading about Neil Peart and enjoying his lyrics, (which I great admired) I also made the decision to be a lyricist. I had read somewhere that he was called the professor — which we all heard proclaimed by Geddy on All the World's a Stage — because he was a voracious reader. "Okay," I said to myself. "It's time to expand beyond Middle-earth and become a voracious reader like Neil." And so I did, which greatly improved my writing skills, not to mention my vocabulary and imagination. It became my favorite pastime and remains so to this day. I suppose I've read thousands of books by now. For many, many years it seemed the decision to make my living as a musician might have been the wrong one. But it worked out well by my thirties with only a handful of people to thank for it. I'll thank Rush now! Loved them at sixteen — love them at sixty![7]*

Perhaps one of the best summaries of the man, though, comes not from a professional musician but from a professional reviewer and writer, Stephen Humphries.

For most drummers, their kit consists of a bass drum, a couple of snares, a hi-hat, and some cymbals. Perhaps a cowbell if they're feeling fancy (and willing to put up with the likelihood that someone in the audience will impersonate Christopher Walken in the SNL sketch by yelling out, well, you know ...). By contrast, Neil Peart surrounded himself with such a complex circular configuration of percussion — from electronic pads to kettle drums to orchestra chimes — that it's a wonder he didn't have to be airlifted in and out of the configuration. Neil approached living much the same way he did his instrument. Not content to be ordinary or conventional, he arrayed himself with out-of-the-ordinary life experiences. Neil truly was a Renaissance Man. He was naturally interested in the world around him and pursued his many interests with hard-working zeal and a disciplined pursuit of excellence. He will be remembered primarily, of course, as one of the greatest drummers ever. But for many of his fans, Neil's approach to living a worthy life is also a large part of his legacy. He didn't just master timing as a drummer. He was a master of time in his daily activities. Not one to squander moments, he'd ask himself, "What's the most excellent thing I can do today?" As a man of letters—including a love of letter-writing—the Canadian musician documented his numerous adventures, exploits, and interests in his books and essays. He took up rowing, swimming, cross-country skiing, bicycling, and motorcycle riding. In each pursuit, he worked to become as proficient as possible in their proper techniques, stretching himself to the limits with his self-described capacity for endurance. A mutual friend of Neil's told me, "He could have been a professional race car driver—his reflexes were that good behind the wheel." Then, too, he was skilled in the culinary arts. An avid birdwatcher. A model-kit builder. A voracious reader. And, most of all, he was a gifted travel writer. His global travelogues were thoughtful treatises about many aspects of life. Despite being famously shy—well beyond reticence—his writings bared his soul. Geddy and Alex may have been relatively more accessible to meeting fans, but it was Neil that followers of the group knew more intimately than his bandmates. Those who personally interacted with the drummer—as I did over several interviews and one indelible studio recording session—will remember him as a genial raconteur with a great sense of humor. For a great many Neil Peart acolytes, his innate curiosity and willingness to try experiences beyond his comfort zone remains an inspiration. When Neil passed on, he was only in his 60s. Yet as someone observed, he'd lived the lives of 10 men. The phrase, "marching to one's own drum" seems as if had been tailor-made to describe Neil Peart.[8]

---

1. Budofsky, *Modern Drummer Legends: Rush's Neil Peart*, 3.
2. Jeff Giles, "Drummer Mike Portnoy Talks Rush Influence in Exclusive Video," *Ultimate Classic Rock* (http://ultimateclassicrock.com/mike-portnoy-video-interview/), April 10, 2015.
3. Mike Portnoy, "*Vapor Trails* Japanese Release Linernotes Essay," April 2002.
4. Robin Armstrong to author, personal correspondence, January 20, 2015.

5. Matt Stevens to author, personal correspondence, May 17, 2015.
6. Andy Tillison to author, personal correspondence, April 28, 2015.
7. Steve Babb to author, personal correspondence, April 14, 2021.
8. Stephen Humphries to author, personal correspondence, April 15, 2021.

ACKNOWLEDGMENTS

I owe a number of fine folks a huge thanks for their help with all of my ideas regarding Peart and Rush.

First and foremost, I thank Kevin McCormick, Erik Heter, Tad Wert, Steve Horwitz (RIP), Steve Hayward, Carl Olson, Paul Moreno, Mark Kalthoff, Scot Bertram, Stephen Humphries, Larry Arnn, Rick Krueger, Rob Olson, Ivan Pongracic, John J. Miller, Pete Blum, Andrew Craske, Paul Watson, Mahesh Sreekandath, Jay Watson, Tom Woods, James Joseph, Dave Bandana, Jeff Deist, and Dom DiGiovanni. A special thanks to my wife, Dedra, Steve, Andrew, Kevin, and Tad for proofreading an early draft of the manuscript and offering lots of good commentary and reflection. Kevin Anderson, Kevin McCormick, and Tad gave the second edition a thorough read as well.

Second, I'd like to thank my great friends, editors, and publishers Kevin J. Anderson and Rebecca Moesta. I admire their skills as much as I cherish their friendship.

Third, I must happily thank Eric Hansen, editor and archivist of *2112.net/powerwindows*. His diligent and careful transcriptions of nearly every article written by or about Rush is boggling to the mind and soul. His good work saved me hundreds of hours of researching in the musty magazine storage warehouses across North America.

Evernote allowed me to collect, store, and sort that research.

And, finally, I thank my wife, Dedra, and my kids—Nathaniel, Gretchen, Maria Grace, Harry, Cecilia Rose (RIP), John Augustine, and Veronica Rose—all of whom have not only put up with my love of all things Rush but who have also encouraged it and joined me in celebrating the band and its art. My wife, especially, has done what she can—rather beautifully and lovingly—to understand my own admiration of Neil Peart. She copy-edited this second edition of the book.

ABOUT THE AUTHOR

Bradley J. Birzer holds the Russell Amos Kirk Chair in American Studies and is Professor of History at Hillsdale College, Michigan. In 2010, he co-founded The Imaginative Conservative website, and, in addition to writing a weekly column, serves as Editor at Large. He also writes for Spirit of Cecilia, Ignatius Insight, Acton, Catholic World Report, and his personal website, Stormfields. In 1990, he earned his B.A. from the University of Notre Dame, and, in 1998, he earned his PhD from Indiana University. He and his wife (Dedra) have seven children, five cats, and one dog.

For the 2014–2015 school year, Birzer held the positions of "Scholar in Residence" and "Visiting Scholar in Conservative Thought and Policy," University of Colorado-Boulder. Birzer cherishes human liberty and dignity; baking; cooking; playing Legos with his kids; hiking and backpacking; good writing; Great Books and Great Ideas; western civilization; science fiction; Apple products; and progressive rock and progressive jazz.

IF YOU LIKED ...

IF YOU LIKED *CULTURAL REPERCUSSIONS*, YOU MIGHT ALSO ENJOY:

Clockwork Angels
Clockwork Lives
Drumbeats
Clockwork Angels: The Comic Scripts

Our list of other WordFire Press authors and titles is always growing. To find out more and to shop our selection of titles, visit us at:
wordfirepress.com

facebook.com/WordfireIncWordfirePress
twitter.com/WordFirePress
instagram.com/WordFirePress
bookbub.com/profile/4109784512

www.ingramcontent.com/pod-product-compliance
Lightning Source LLC
Chambersburg PA
CBHW071239070526
44583CB00017B/2249